BRUCE WEBER
THROUGH MY EYES

An Inside Look At The Man, The Coach And
The Greatest Season In Illinois History

By BRUCE WEBER
with MARK TUPPER

KCI SPORTS VENTURES, LLC
SAVOY, IL

CREDITS

Front cover photo courtesy of Mark Jones/Illinois Sports Information Office.

ISBN: 0-9758769-4-5

Published By:

KCI Sports Ventures, LLC

1402 Quail Run Drive

Savoy, IL 61874

Publisher: Peter J. Clark

Coordinating Editor: Molly Voorheis

Cover Design: Terry Neutz Hayden

Book Layout and Design: Terry Neutz Hayden

Sales & Marketing: Bret D. Kroencke

Photos courtesy of Mark Jones/Illinois Sports Information Office and the family of Bruce Weber. Gene Keady photo courtesy of Purdue Sports Information Office. Mark Tupper photo courtesy of *Decatur Herald & Review.*

Printed and bound by Worzalla Publishing, Stevens Point, WI.

BRUCE WEBER WITH MARK TUPPER

DEDICATION

For my late parents, Stan and Eileen Tupper. They would have loved this team and this season and I would have loved sharing the journey with them.

Mark Tupper

For my parents, Louis and Dawn Weber.

Bruce Weber

ACKNOWLEDGEMENTS

I'd like to thank the "Sportswriter Prom" crew of John Supinie, Herb Gould, Jim Benson and Jeremy Rutherford along with a host of guests who joined us to make this memorable season even more enjoyable, including Bernie Miklasz, Marlen Garcia, Loren Tate, Lindsey Wilhite, Mike Imren, Steve Batterson, Mike Albright, Kelly Huff, Don Doxsie, Prince Steve Overbey, Gary Childs, Jeff Shelman, Kent Brown, Derrick Burson, Cassie Arner, Steve Bardo, Ryan Baker, Tim Cain, Vahe Gregorian, Brian Barnhart, Ed Bond, Steve Kelly, Brian Hanley, Rob Schultz, Melissa Issacson, Jay Adande, Bob Baptist, Bruce Hooley, Phil Arvia, Nick Pietruszkiewicz, Dan Roan, Jim Turpin, Tim Cronin, Mike Pearson, Dave Wilhelm, Steve Porter, Matt Trowbridge, Jeff Wendland, Mike Nadel, Bill Liesse, Greg Stewart, Kirk Wessler, Jim Ruppert, Brett Dawson, Dave Loane, Fowler Connell, Chad Dare, Jason Elliott, Andrew Miller, Rob Collins, Tom McNamara, Brandon Blocker, Steve Breitwieser, Eric Loy, Mike Cleff, Jim Cotter and, conspicuous by her absence, Erin Andrews. And to Cindy Butkovich, the all-knowing gatekeeper of the Illini basketball operation.

Mark Tupper

FOREWORD

Talk about an awkward start to a relationship. When Bruce Weber first came to see me about a graduate assistant job at Western Kentucky, I wasn't even there. I had been asked to appear on short notice by USA Basketball, so I never got to meet the young coach. My assistant coaches at the time, Clem Haskins and Ray Hite, interviewed him. Both spoke highly of him, so I thought we'd bring him in for another interview. When Bruce told me from a pay phone in some high school gym in Wisconsin where he was working a basketball camp that he didn't have the money to drive back to Western, I decided to hire him over the phone. I'm glad I did.

People often ask me, "What did you see in him?" What I saw was a basketball junkie, an extremely hard worker, and a person who was going to be very loyal. Bruce has always been a tremendous detail guy. You didn't have to tell him what to do, he just did it. We had a saying in our program–fly a jet–which means to think ahead. Bruce was always flying a jet.

Assistants didn't make much back in those days, so Megan (Bruce's wife) supplemented his income by being a nurse. We were putting in long hours during the season and then would hit the road for recruiting. I think sometimes coaches have a tendency to take family for granted. It is not fair to the family, but it happens with the hours that are required to be a successful Division I coach. Bruce has always been fortunate to have a great family. In a way, we grew up together. We saw all of the Weber children born in West Lafayette . . . . the Weber's were like relation, but better than relation because they weren't actually relation! They didn't want or expect anything. His three girls are great kids. They are like nieces to my wife and I.

Watching Illinois make their great run to the national championship game this year was quite an experience. It was as if I was pulling for my own team. I was very proud of their accomplishments. I couldn't be prouder of or happier for Bruce. We have always had a special relationship. As I watched him coach during the Final Four, I couldn't help but think back to the day he arrived in Bowling Green, Kentucky and just how far he had come. I was very fortunate, some might say lucky, to have had him as my assistant for 18 years.

This book is a fitting tribute to the coach and players whose accomplishments over the past season have made a university and state proud. I hope you enjoy looking back on a very special Illini season.

Gene Keady
Head Basketball Coach, Purdue University
1980-2005

BRUCE WEBER WITH MARK TUPPER

CONTENTS

CHAPTER ONE

THE PAIN AND THE PLEDGE

It was a warm Friday evening in late March, and the kind of balmy spring breeze that routinely kisses the South danced through the streets of Atlanta. College basketball fans floated along with it, carried to the northwest edge of downtown by high hopes and a growing feeling of excitement.

Deep inside the festive Georgia Dome, University of Illinois basketball Coach Bruce Weber waited in the team's locker room, checking through the scouting report, reviewing the individual matchups and thinking about the preparation that had brought his team to this point.

"At first you look at the Duke stuff and you think, 'Wow, we can't beat them.' But then you talk to some coaches and you look at some more tape, and you think, 'Yeah, we have a chance. We can play with them. We can beat them.'"

BRUCE WEBER WITH MARK TUPPER

Duke. No coincidence that the name is synonymous with college basketball royalty. And nearing the end of this 2003-04 season, Coach Mike Krzyzewski had brought the Blue Devils down to Georgia as a No. 1 seed in the NCAA Tournament, playing in their seventh consecutive Sweet 16, looking for a fourth national championship since 1991. Duke doesn't just show up at an NCAA Tournament. It regally parades into the field, as though it is waiting for a coronation. And despite an opponent's declaration to the contrary, playing Duke as a top seed is a daunting and intimidating assignment.

No one knows it at the time, but less than a year from now Duke starters Luol Deng and Chris Duhon will be starting for the Chicago Bulls. And on this night Illinois will have to contend with both dynamic inside player Shelden Williams, who Weber has worried about all week, and one of the game's most dangerous shooters, J.J. Redick. Beating Duke is always a tall order, but that's particularly true in the heightening fervor of this setting. And it is this setting that has Weber concerned right now.

Oh, he has plenty of confidence in his team. And he's so, so proud of them. In less than 11 months, since April 30, 2003, when he was hired as Illinois' 16th men's head basketball coach, Weber and this group have navigated a tricky and sometimes painful path. But they've made it here together, growing day by day, struggling through the transition every new coach faces while encountering more hurdles than anyone could have imagined.

Weber soothed hurt feelings from players stung by the departure of a popular coach. He dealt with difficulties adapting to a new offense, a new defensive commitment and a stepped-up level of conditioning. Distracting off-court issues stemmed from a campus burglary. And, of course, there was the ever-present impatience of fans demanding immediate results.

Together they dealt with issues Weber couldn't have fathomed. They won over fans who were skeptical of his motion offense, of his never-compromising man-to-man defense, of his wardrobe that favored sport coats over suits, of his gravelly voice and his disarming honesty. In a courageous burst they won 10 in a row to close out the regular season, locking up Illinois' first outright Big Ten Conference championship in 52 years. Six of those victories came on the road. And just five days earlier, No. 13 Illinois had advanced to this Sweet 16 showdown by leveling 11th-ranked Cincinnati 92-68, shooting 63.6 percent and totally de-clawing the Bearcats. The win marked the first time in university history Illinois had defeated a higher tournament seed.

But the intensity rises when teams reach the Sweet 16 round of the NCAA Tournament, and Weber knew stepping into the vast Georgia Dome could have its own imposing impact. After a final talk with his team, the Illini players and assistant coaches headed for the floor. Weber, as always, remained behind a moment longer. Then he slipped on his coat, went to the restroom, and used the mirror to adjust his necktie. He washed his hands, took a deep, even breath and strode alone from the locker room, briskly making the long walk into the vast, vibrating arena. He didn't like what he sensed from the start.

"You could feel it when we walked out there," he said. "You're in a dome, it's the awe of being there on that huge stage, Duke has been there and we really haven't. And when you walk out there it really hits you. It's like, 'Oh-oh, we're really here.'

"I know our guys were feeling it and they also had it in their heads that it's harder to shoot in a dome. They remembered what happened the year before in Indianapolis, when they lost to Notre Dame in the second round of the Tournament."

What happened in the RCA Dome on the final day of Illinois' 2003 season was a 34.9 percent shooting disaster that contributed to Illinois' 68-60 loss to the Fighting Irish. "So they walk out there against Duke thinking it's hard to shoot in a dome. The crazy thing was, Notre Dame made 13 3's that same day. Well, how the heck can they shoot like that and you can't?"

Logic does not always have a place in the NCAA Tournament. And after the ball was tipped, Weber quickly had to deal with two disturbing developments. "We started out good but right away we get two quick fouls on Deron (Williams) and two on James

(Augustine). Those are the two people we can't lose. James because of defense and Deron because of his solid play. Deron was coming off scoring 31 against Cincinnati and if you look at Deron's numbers against Duke you can see he never got back into the game.

"Even so, we're still in it. But Luther (Head) misses a layup, we miss some other layups and just don't take advantage of our opportunities." When it was over - after Illinois' season ended with a 72-62 loss - Weber made the long walk back to the team's locker room thinking about what he'd say. He was disappointed, obviously, even a little mad, mainly because he knew he was correct in his assessment that Illinois could have beaten Duke. But he also recognized this as a chance to begin a much greater quest. And after pushing through the locker room doors, he made that point clear to his players.

"After I got them in the locker room, I said, 'Everyone is going to say we have all our guys back, but you know that's not true," he said, his eyes fixing on the only senior, Jerrance Howard. "I asked them, 'Who's going to replace Jerrance?' Jerrance was such a glue guy. He was the liaison between the coaches and the players, and he helped us through all of the tough times. He was there for the guys when they were in trouble.

"When we had guys suspended, he actually played and had his career high in minutes. Then when those guys came back he just sat down and didn't say a word. He enjoyed the whole thing, just being part of it."

"And that was the thing I challenged them on. 'It starts right now, right here. You guys have a taste of it. You're hungry. Do you want more? Do you want more?'" Everyone in the room already did.

Slumped back into his locker stall, Luther Head looked racked with a combination of regret and exhaustion. No player had gone through more personal travails than Head, and his dream for this game did not include a 4-for-11 shooting night that produced just nine points. But as he sat there and mentally regrouped, he seemed to begin focusing on the promise of his coach's message. "We became a family this season," Head said, "and we feel good about us."

It's always sad when a promising season ends. But with all contributing players due to return, with maturity moved up a notch, with the challenges of a first year together behind them at last, and with Weber's message already taking seed, this moment felt more like a beginning than an end. In a few months Bruce Weber and his players would discover if that was true.

CHAPTER TWO

GROWING UP BRUCE

Who's to say what constitutes a childhood of riches? If it's the size
of your house, Bruce Weber was poor. If it's the trendy fashions
hanging in your closet, he was poor. If it's the lavish trips your family takes, he was poor. And if it's the size of the family bank account,
he was very poor indeed.

But from the day he was born - October 19, 1956 - Bruce Brett
Weber had the feeling he was a lucky kid who landed in an embar-
rassment of riches. His father, Louis Weber, came to America by
boat from Austria when he was just a toddler. The Weber family settled in Milwaukee where Louie's parents spoke German. Louie
Weber's father was a tailor, a very strict man it was best not to mess
with. Louie's mother was known as an incredible cook. It was in
Milwaukee where Louie Weber would eventually meet the woman he
would marry, Dawn Protzmann, who was born in the upper peninsula of Michigan and whose mother, a Johnston, was Swedish.

"My dad worked for Heil Co., which makes dump trucks, then got a second job at the A&P," Bruce Weber recalled. "He was like a distributor for truck parts. He did a little sales, but when people needed parts, he was the guy. He was a guy who just kind of slinked through school. He was a good athlete and he loved to play basketball. He also helped run the rec centers in our area. He opened the gyms and supervised the playgrounds. Heck, he played basketball until he was 60 years old.

"He was a street smart person - not book smart - but street smart, and his whole life was people. He loved talking. He'd be on the phone with you forever. We got tickets to basketball games and Notre Dame football games. My dad talked to everybody. Everybody was Louie's buddy. That was his life. Even my friends, they called him Louie and they loved to come to the house and talk with him, just to hear his stories. He just dealt with people very, very well. And he looked like Al McGuire," Weber said, referring to the legendary Marquette University basketball coach. "He'd be closing up one of the rec centers and was supposed to be home at 9, but at 9:30 he was still there just talking with someone. That's how he was, always talking."

It probably was easier to be buddies with Louie Weber if you were not one of his three sons or two daughters. "My relationship with him was good, but at the same time he was tough on us. As you get older, it's more about respect. But he was tough. He didn't beat us or anything, but I got spanked. That's how it was in that day and age. I had a couple of buddies who didn't have dads in their life, and they liked to come over and listen to his philosophy of life."

His philosophy definitely included a love for sports, all sports, but especially basketball. And at a young age Bruce Weber embraced sports as a major part of his life. "My life was such a simple life. I went to the playground every single day. I didn't know any better. I played basketball until it got dark and when it got dark we went to someone's house and played in their driveway. Or we went and got a pizza. And that was it."

OK, there was a little more to it than that. Louie Weber and a man named Tom Desotel, who Weber still regards as a close friend, started a youth basketball team they called the Whiz Kids. "It's kind of amazing how it transpired and the link to the name of the Whiz Kids team at Illinois," Bruce Weber said, referring to the storied Illini squad of the early 1940s. "Tom ran a lot of the summer playground leagues. That's where he and my dad got involved. It was junior high kids and he coached all of us in junior high. He created this team and we traveled around Milwaukee playing. The Catholic schools and the Lutheran schools had teams and leagues for kids, but that was it in Milwaukee at that time. The public schools didn't have anything.

"But the rec centers would have leagues on Saturday mornings, so my dad coached my older brother, Ron, and then me, and they started it for several different age groups. It was kind of the beginning of AAU a long time ago. We would go into an African-American area, a black community, and we might have been the only white team that ever played there. My dad thought it was so important, not only the competition, but seeing and understanding race and being exposed to something else. Now, when I think about it, it was amazing at that time." In those turbulent times, racial tension was very much a part of the inner-city landscape. "I remember the riots we had in the 60's in Milwaukee. You weren't supposed to leave your house. We went to the park to play and the police told us to go home. There was looting in downtown Milwaukee."

Throughout the family's three-bedroom house at 72nd Street, six blocks from the John Marshall High School the five Weber children would attend, there was a constant buzz of activity and much of it centered on sports. Only Louie Weber's devotion to sports and the willingness, patience and understanding of Dawn Weber, who still talked in her Upper Peninsula 'Ya, hey' dialect, could have allowed the Weber household to be ruled by such chaos.

"Everyone loved to come to our house because you could do anything you wanted in our house. In the winter we would set up a basketball court in the basement. I was a little kid and we taped the lines on the floor and we played. One time I did a jump shot and there was this metal beam in the ceiling, and I just cracked the heck out of my head and busted it open. Big stitches. Then it would become spring and usually on spring break we would play a game called strikeout in the basement with Whiffle balls. You could throw as hard as you wanted and they could hit it as hard as they wanted. If it went past the pitcher it was a single. If it went above one line on the wall it was a double. Above another line it was a triple. Above the top line and it was a home run. I just remember growing up playing strikeout and listening to the Brewers or Braves on the radio. That's kind of how we did it.

"Even in the hallways, we always played basketball. We played football on our knees in the living room. The mom of one of our cousin's had passed away from cancer, and we kind of took her in. She said when the weekends came and knew she had to go some-where, she prayed she could go to our house because she knew she could jump on the beds and all that stuff. We'd knock over furni-ture and sometimes break stuff, but my mom just kind of went along with it."

Games were always at the center of the family's attention and even Bruce's mother, who took a job at the local J.C. Penney's and worked in virtually every department, had an appreciation for the role this activity played in their family. "We loved going to games," Bruce Weber said. "We went to high school basketball games, to Marquette games, to any game we could get a ticket for. When the Milwaukee Bucks first came along, you could go for a dollar. They had this 'Buck Night for the Bucks' at certain games, and one year I saw like 30 games. My dad was always talking to people who had tickets. Packer games were a little harder, but I still remember going to Lambeau Field when I was a young kid. Once I got to go to an Illinois football game at Notre Dame. It was like 51-0 or 57-0. I said something to Mr. Guenther about it and, yes, he remembered the game." Most likely it was Notre Dame's 58-8 victory on October 19, 1968, Bruce Weber's 12th birthday.

"And when we weren't going to a game in person, we were listening on the radio or were watching on TV. I still remember my first game (on television), watching in black and white. It was Kentucky vs. UTEP (in 1966), which was Texas Western then, in the national championship game. The picture was real fuzzy, on channel 18, our independent station. That was my first recollection of a Final Four game. And I always watched the Big Ten 'Game of the Week' on

Saturday.

"I listened to Marquette games and Wisconsin games on the radio, whether it was football or basketball. And in basketball, we always kept our own scorecard for the game. I remember a couple of times they'd play a West Coast game, and I'd sneak the transistor radio into bed. I had an earphone and my mom would think I was asleep. I'd listen to Marquette play Air Force or San Francisco with a sheet of paper and a flashlight." Not bad since Bruce, Ron and David Weber all shared one bedroom. Jan and Carrie Weber, the sisters, shared another, while the parents, Louie and Dawn Weber, had the third.

The time Bruce Weber split his head open on the basement beam was not an aberration. He was a familiar face at the local hospital. "I was the one who was kind of the black sheep. Not in a bad way, but I was always getting hurt. My mom always had to watch me. I was a little reckless. I had it figured out one time; I was in the emergency room 17 times by the time I was 14 years old. I was running into walls, twice I got hit by cars, I caught a fly ball in the outfield and came down on top of a jagged chain link fence. It went into my side and ripped a chunk of skin out of me.

"I played baseball and I was a catcher. I was always in the action. I was not as talented as I was tough, but I was pretty aggressive. I loved the contact and the action, and I took a pounding. I was riding my bike one time and, Bam! I got hit by a car and ended up on the front windshield. I still remember being smashed against the windshield. One time I was going to the store to get popcorn. It was my dad's vacation and we were going to the drive-in theater. So I took the shortcuts through the alleys and I got hit by a car. I was all bloody, but we were going to the drive-in so I wasn't going to tell anybody. I went to the store to get the popcorn, and the people who hit me followed me back home because they were afraid I wouldn't tell my parents. I ended up having to go to the emergency room anyway.

"I had to wear a body cast before my sophomore or junior year in high school. I had a slipped disc and a cracked vertebrae. At the time they didn't do surgery, or if they were going to do it they said it was a major thing. They just felt a body cast might realign everything. They said it was just from the constant pounding of being a catcher. Like I said, when I played sports I was a little reckless."

Weber also dreamed of playing football. His older brother, Ron, was a quarterback at John Marshall High School but suffered a broken leg in consecutive seasons. "I came up wanting to play, too, but my parents said, 'No way.' Not with my history."

Love - not money - kept the Weber family together. "We were middle class. We made it, but we sure didn't save. We didn't go on any big vacations. A big vacation was going to Chicago for a White Sox or Cubs game. Or we went to the Dells. Everyone in Wisconsin goes to the Dells. Christmas was my favorite holiday, by far, and the one thing my parents did save for was Christmas. Dad had a Christmas club at work, and he put money aside each month. They were always sure at Christmas our house would be full of presents. They may not have been huge, expensive things, but we always got lots of stuff."

The best Christmas gifts, of course, had something to do with sports. "Electric football was one of the best. And there was this basketball card game where you could buy leagues or teams, NBA or college, and it would be Pete Maravich and you'd spin this thing and we played it all the time. It was like the initial version of PlayStation. There was strategy and the whole thing was we got to learn so much about teams and players. We thought it was the greatest."

Other kids may have lived in more affluent neighborhoods and spent their summers vacationing in faraway places. But in the Weber household, there was always the sound of busy, happy children. "We were happy," Bruce Weber said. "We didn't know any different." Years later, Ron Weber, the oldest son, would become head basketball coach at Waupaca High School in east-central Wisconsin. David Weber, the youngest of the Weber boys, would become head basketball coach at Glenbrook North High School in suburban Chicago. And Bruce Weber would become the head basketball coach at the University of Illinois. Given their upbringing, and with so much tolerance and support from their parents, is it any wonder?

CHAPTER THREE

SETTING THE BAR

It was only a matter of days after the loss to Duke in Atlanta that
Bruce Weber picked up his phone and called the Missouri Valley
Conference office in St. Louis. "I told them I wanted to give our
players a St. Louis Final Four T-shirt and wanted to know if I could
use the logo. The Valley was going to be hosting the Final Four, and
they said it was fine as long as I wasn't selling it and just doing it for
our team. I wanted it to be our spring workout shirt."

Immediately after Weber was hired at Illinois, his players talked
about getting to the 2004 Final Four in San Antonio. Weber wanted
to set the bar high, but he didn't rush to embrace that goal for a
variety of reasons.

"To be honest, that first year I didn't think we were ready for the
Final Four. We'd lost Brian Cook and I didn't know if we had a go-
to guy. I didn't know if we had the maturity. I said, 'You guys are

talking about the Final Four, but you didn't even get by the second round (with the loss to Notre Dame). We have to get by the second round before we can talk about the Final Four.'

"As it turned out, we got to the Sweet 16 and maybe it's a deal where if you reach that goal, guys stop there. I don't know if that's the deal, but it has happened to me a couple of times."

During his 18 seasons as an assistant coach at Purdue, Weber doesn't remember his boss and mentor Gene Keady dangling goals like the Final Four. "Never goals that high. Most of the time our goal was to win the Big Ten championship," something Purdue accomplished six times during the Keady-Weber run. "The Purdue team with Troy Lewis, we were good enough to get to the Final Four, but we'd never been there and we didn't understand it. You get to the Dome, the Sweet 16, and the same thing happened to us that happened when (Illinois) played Duke. We played Kansas State that year (in 1988 in the Pontiac Silverdome). We wanted to get there, we expected to get there, but all of a sudden you're tight and it took a toll on us."

It was after Weber left Purdue in 1998, accepting his first head coaching stint at Southern Illinois University, that he saw the value in challenging players by setting the bar high.

"The one year I thought we were going to be pretty good (2001-02), I put it on the board. I said, 'Here are your goals: Missouri Valley Conference championship, NCAA Tournament,' and I added one more, 'Sweet 16.'

"We had played Mississippi the year before in Hawaii and should have beaten them (SIU lost, 70-66). We led the whole way. And that was the year Mississippi slipped into the Sweet 16. So I asked them, 'Should we have beaten them? Yes. Could we have? Yes. Well, now we're going to be better. We're adding Rolan Roberts. Why can't we be in their place?'" As the season played out, Weber forgot about adding "Sweet 16" to his list of goals. But his players did not.

"The next season we beat Indiana and all of a sudden we're getting this attention. And the kids were being interviewed on national TV, and they said, 'Coach said we should be in the Sweet 16.' And I'm going, 'Oh, God, why did I say that?'

"But that got it in their minds. And that was the year we beat Texas Tech and Georgia to make it to the Sweet 16. I learned not to be afraid to set the bar high if I felt it was something we could do."

So after placing a call to the Missouri Valley Conference regarding use of the Final Four logo, Weber went to work. As a fifth-grade teacher in Wisconsin, he had seen the value of using incentives and motivational devices to trigger positive responses from his students. That's why he makes up T-shirts with inspirational messages. That's why he writes motivational buzz words on the team's message board before practices and games, using blue and orange markers and red stars.

That's why he and assistant coaches Gary Nottingham and Wayne McClain dredge up phrases and catchy thoughts for players to digest. And that's why he still hands out suckers as rewards. "I know who likes Jolly Rancher, Starburst and Blow Pops. And if Deron Williams doesn't get the right sucker, he gets mad."

Passing out candy treats was something Weber picked up at Southern Illinois, where he'd hand them out the night before a game. The budget was tight and he'd swoop up sacks of half-priced candy the day after Halloween or Christmas or Easter and store them in his desk. He was amazed at how much the players looked forward to the sugary snacks. Jack Ingram loved Jolly Rancher. Deron Williams liked chocolate, so Weber would bring in miniature Snickers and Kit-Kat bars. "Dee Brown had all those cavities and yet he'd take more candy than anyone. (Trainer) Al Martindale accused me of promoting bad dental care."

Just two weeks after the loss to Duke, Weber ordered up the T-shirts. "On the front I had the St. Louis Final Four logo. And on the back I put 100th Anniversary, Illini Basketball Family Reunion, St. Louis, Mo., April 2-4.'

"And then we put the Final Four logo up in our locker room right away. I was saying, 'OK, this is a special year. Let's go for it.'"

The summer was the time to find out who would replace Jerrance Howard. "We always talk about the true captain, the true leader, he's the one who leads when the coaches aren't around. And we can't be with them over the summer.

"We had very good individual workouts in the spring. And in our team meeting I challenged them. I said, 'Somebody is not going to be happy. We have everyone back. And Warren Carter is going to be a year older. Rich McBride is going to be a year older. We can't play everybody, so somebody is going to be unhappy. You'd better realize it and take it to heart. Because the guy who doesn't work hard is going to get passed by. And you're going to be mad at me when you should be mad at yourself for letting it slip by.'"

It was a message that would help set the tone for an entire season.

"Jack Ingram, Luther Head and Roger Powell took it to heart. That was one thing Coach Keady always said, that your seniors need to have the best year of their careers to be really special. And they took it to heart. Obviously, the one person who didn't and struggled all year was Nick (Smith). He didn't step it up a level like the other guys. He actually did give a little more effort than he normally did, but it still wasn't what everybody else did.

"The whole point was, it was competition, there was a fear factor and it drove some guys to step up their game and go to another level."

Weber's hope was that each player would find improvement in some aspect of his individual game and that it would translate into an improved team game.

"Hopefully, with what we do - the drill work, the individual stuff - when you do it for a full year, then going into the second year you really get the benefit of it. And if they can do it on their own when they get into the gym in the summer, that can really help.

"One thing I talked to Luther about was not always taking a back seat to Deron and Dee. But what he said really hit me. He said, 'I agree with you coach, but they're off at Nike, they're off at USA Basketball, they're off at Michael Jordan's camp. And I'm in Champaign.'

"So I said, 'That doesn't mean you have to take a back seat to them. You can work your butt off here to make the strides you need to get better. They may be playing and getting some other stuff, but you can't give in.' And he didn't."

It was later that summer when Weber began to realize how the rest of the country was coming to view the 2004-05 Fighting Illini basketball team. "I remember I was driving on July 7th, the first day of recruiting, going to Indianapolis. I actually got two calls that day. The first one was from Brian Cardinal (who played for Keady and Weber at Purdue). He was negotiating his contract with the (NBA) Memphis Grizzlies. He called and said, 'Coach, what do you think I'm worth?'

I said, 'Probably more than they're going to give you.'

"Brian said, 'What are you doing?' I told him I was driving to Indy. "Well, Coach, you'd better pull over.' Then he said, 'Do you think I should accept $37 million?' I nearly went off the road."

The next phone call gave Weber a jolt, too. "It was a guy from Athlon (magazine) and he said they were thinking about putting us No. 1 in their pre-season issue. He wanted to know how I felt about that. At first I was like, 'Golly, I don't want that.' But the more I thought about it, it's good for the program, it's good for the kids. Everyone is going to expect us to be great anyway, so why not say that? It's the old Lou Holtz crying stuff, then everyone makes fun of you anyway.

"Then Playboy called, and they said they were making us No.1, too. I liked it, but there was a little fear involved, no doubt."

It was a designation Illinois would become used to. Ranked pre-season No. 1 in two magazines was only the start.

CHAPTER FOUR

POT HOLES

If there was another surprise in the off-season spring and summer of 2004 it began with a phone call Weber received, this one while unpacking boxes in his garage. The Weber family's whirlwind move from Carbondale to Champaign had been a hectic fast break and more than a year later they were still shuffling boxes and rearranging their lives as they finally settled into their newly built brick home.

It was not, as Bruce and Megan Weber first hoped, situated out in the country, amid the woods and wide open spaces. But it afforded them enough space to breathe and a winding, beautiful, low-traffic street on which to share their morning walks with dogs Daisy and Penny, a time Weber cherishes and uses to clear his mind and catch up on all the things a husband and best friend may let slip by the wayside when he is charging through the rest of his 16-hour work day.

"I remember I got the call while I was sweating out in the garage, and it was one of our beat reporters wanting to know if I'd like to comment on Roger (Powell)." The call caught Weber off guard. Oh, sure, he'd had a conversation with his senior-to-be forward about his professional basketball aspirations. But news that Powell had submitted his name for the National Basketball Association's early-entry draft list blind-sided him.

"I had no idea. I said I'd have to call Roger and then let him know. I couldn't even hang up the phone and it was Andy Katz (from ESPN.com) and he's saying the same thing." As it turned out, Powell and his family felt the strategy might bring him some exposure and get NBA types thinking about the powerfully built Joliet native, who might have been Illinois' best player on the floor in the season-ending loss to Duke. And even though Powell would withdraw his name and return for his senior year, Weber suddenly understood he'd need to confront "the NBA thing" head-on. "I realized, 'Golly, we have to worry about this stuff already.'"

He'd also had preliminary conversations with guards Deron

Williams and Dee Brown, getting a read on their thoughts. Both intended to return for their junior seasons, something Weber was counting on. But after the Powell surprise, well....

"I really started to investigate it. I did a lot of stuff. And one thing that happened came about because of Coach Turner," he said, referring to the former Illini head football coach, Ron Turner. "We have to give a lot of talks, and I went with Coach Turner and he talked about the year after the Sugar Bowl and how he'd had some pretty good players drafted off that team. He said the beginning of the next season they were so screwed up because so many of his main players were all worried about their agents, where they were going to go in the draft, and the team thing was totally secondary. I just thought, 'God, I can't let that happen.'

"I knew we had an upperclass-oriented team, our seniors would be thinking about it and our juniors were thinking about it, too. Deron and Dee and I had already talked about it and then we had the Roger thing. And, I hoped, Luther would be someone who would get on the NBA's radar screen, too."

While some coaches might choose to push all NBA talk into the background, Weber decided it best to bring it to the front.

"I talked to our team about who makes all-Big Ten and the all-America teams. If you go through them, the all-Big Ten guys are almost always from teams who finish one-two-three, and there's usually the other guy who shoots every time for the bad team. And the guys who make the all-America teams are from teams ranked in the top 10 or top 20 for most of the year. I talked to them about using that publicity to help them. I said, 'Don't let your individual focus interfere with our team. If our team does well, you'll get the opportunities,' never imagining what would happen.

"The thing is, they all did get attention. So our team's performance really helped. Somebody joked that I would never mention Dee without saying something about Deron. And I added Luther into the mix, too. No matter who anyone said, I'd mention all three because I didn't want that to be a factor with them. No matter what, we're all human, they all have egos, they all have parents and grandparents and cousins and girlfriends, so sooner or later there's going to be some of that jealousy in there.

"And then I brought in Stan Kasten (former president of the Atlanta Hawks). He talked to our team about what the pros are looking for. He said that obviously they are looking for the best players. But all of the intangibles come into play. If you have success as a team, you're going to get noticed. It was a great message. If you have success you'll have people watching you. The further you go, the more attention you'll get. When you get to the Sweet 16, there are four games on Thursday night and four on Friday night. Now, if every NBA scout is out, there's a great chance there is one of them at your game. If you get to the Final Four, they're all there.

"The example I used was Rolan Roberts," Weber said, referring to the powerfully built inside player who had helped lead Southern Illinois into the Sweet 16. "I started calling in January about getting him into Portsmouth for the pre-draft camp. They said they were full, that he was on a waiting list, blah, blah, blah. Then we have the run, we go play UConn in the Sweet 16 and Rolan gets 24 and (Emeka) Okafor gets nine. We took it right at Okafor. And even though we lost the game, on Monday morning I have messages all over the place. 'Rolan needs to be in Portsmouth next week. We want Rolan there!' It just showed me what kind of attention you can get if your team does well.

"Deron always jokes that I talk so much, nobody listens. But sooner or later they do listen. They buy in. Some of it goes over their heads, but I knew if we didn't address it and just avoided the whole NBA thing, we'd kick ourselves in the butt later on."

As it turned out, the 2004-05 Illini team would never let dreams of life in the pro's upset dreams of glory in college. Even in those early practice sessions, there was a noticeable difference. "High school coaches at our clinic were all talking about it. They'd say, 'Man, you guys are going so hard.' The thing is, there was competition." And when those tough practices led to exhibition game victories over Southern Illinois-Edwardsville and Lewis, the Illini Express was ready to pull away from the station.

Well, nearly ready. The team received its worst medical news of the season in a practice session following the November 5 victory over SIU-Edwardsville. The victim was Brian Randle, the extraordinary athlete from Peoria for whom Weber had such high hopes.

"First of all, Brian had this shoulder problem the year before when he was a freshman. He played through pain that season. We know he aggravated it in the Indiana game of the Big Ten Tournament. He dove for a ball and landed on his shoulder. He came back and he was crying. There were tears in his eyes. But we think somewhere before that was when he probably first injured it.

"At that time he's a freshman, he's lost his confidence and he hit the wall a little bit, like most freshmen do. We played him a couple minutes here and there, but he was struggling. Then he has surgery after the season ends and the trainers and doctors were amazed that he had played through such pain because it was a major shoulder problem. So he can't do anything all spring, basically most of the summer, and he comes back at the end of July and we know he needs to build a lot of strength.

"Brian came to me right after school started in August and said, 'Coach, I'd probably like to red-shirt.' I said, 'Brian, let's wait and see.' He told me he didn't have his strength or timing. I went back and talked to his family. One of his parents was OK with it and one wasn't. I said let's just wait and see. And I think he just relaxed and started playing. He had great fall workouts. It got to the point where he was playing pretty good and we really thought he could be a factor. He was a defensive stopper off the bench and he brought energy. I thought then with Brian in the mix we wouldn't wear down.

"But at practice after the first exhibition game, he misses a contested jumper and the guy runs down to the other end and Brian tries to block his shot and I call a foul. So now he's frustrated and walks about five feet to the wall and he just kind of pounds the wall. To be honest, a lot of guys do it. But he hit it with his left fist. And even though the wall is padded, he just turns his fist wrong. At first, when I saw him do it, I saw him wince. And I thought maybe he did something to his shoulder again. I told him to go see (trainer) Al (Martindale). And about two minutes later, Al comes running to me and said, 'Brian broke his hand.' I said, 'How did he do it? I saw him hit the wall but it didn't look anything like that.'

"We took him in that night and the X-rays were way worse than anyone could have imagined. With all the small bones in there they had to do surgery and place three pins. They are saying the earliest he could return was mid-January and that's maybe at 75 percent and by then you're losing conditioning. Even before the season we were asked, 'What do you need to make the big run?' And we said, 'Well, we have to avoid injuries.' And here, right away, it pops up even before the season starts, right at a point when Brian was showing us he could really help. And now you think you don't have the depth. Now you have to force Warren (Carter) to play the (small forward) for us where he has trouble guarding 3's. He can shoot and do things on the perimeter like a 3, but he has trouble guarding little quick guys. All of a sudden you're looking around at each other and wondering, 'Is it going to be one of those seasons?'"

CHAPTER FIVE

A NEW BEGINNING

While Brian Randle's broken hand would have a season-long impact on the Illini basketball team, Weber himself made an early-season visit to the injury list.

On Friday, November 12 - exactly one week before the regular-season opener against Delaware State - Weber felt some discomfort on the side of his lower stomach and brought it to the attention of his doctor. "He wanted to get me in right away but my mom was coming for the weekend and I never see her," he said at the time. "I asked for an antibiotic and Monday morning I felt better. Coincidentally, I had to go in for a scan and also for my stress test. He took my temperature, which was normal, and my blood count early was normal. I was on the treadmill for 15 minutes when they called me out and said I had acute appendicitis. They took me to the operating room right off the treadmill."

Surgery to remove his appendix followed. And despite wanting to jump immediately from the operating room back to his office and into the routine of game preparation, Weber realized he'd need to slow down, even if only for a couple days. "The first day you're still drugged up. The next two days are the tough days," he said shortly after the surgery. "I tried to concentrate at home, watching game film, but I kept falling asleep because the Vicodin knocked me out. They punched three holes in me and I feel like a naked turkey before Thanksgiving."

Despite this painful setback, which did not keep Weber from coaching the November 19 opener against Delaware State, it was nothing like the pain he had experienced at this time one year ago.

The Illini basketball world was tossed into upheaval in what came to be known as "the three dominoes" that fell at the end of the 2003 season. Roy Williams' decision to leave the University of Kansas for North Carolina left a huge void in Lawrence, Kan. And when Kansas convinced Bill Self to leave Illinois, the spotlight shifted to the vacancy in Champaign.

Down in Carbondale, where he had just finished his fifth season as head coach at Southern Illinois University, Bruce Weber read accounts of what Illinois Director of Athletics Ron Guenther wanted in a new coach. "I said at the time, 'If that's really what he's looking for then I'm the guy.'" Unbeknownst to Weber, Guenther was already on the phone with Purdue Coach Gene Keady, gathering information about the man who'd been on Guenther's radar for three years. Guenther had seen Weber coach against Illinois in Las Vegas (a game Illinois barely won, 75-72, on November 24, 2001). He'd watched Weber coach the Salukis past Bob Knight and Texas Tech and past Jim Harrick and Georgia into the Sweet 16. And he loved the toughness Keady's Purdue teams brought to the floor every night during the 18 years Weber had been a Boilermaker assistant in West Lafayette, Ind.

Weber said not in his wildest dreams did he imagine he'd one day be coaching in front of the other bench the night his Salukis squared off against Illinois in Vegas. "No, not at all. That was a crazy game." Weber's SIU squad played tough and he coached hard from the sideline, knowing all along how much a victory over Illinois would mean to his players and to Saluki fans. "We had people fly out there just to watch that game," he said. It was only the second time in history the two schools had met, and Illinois' 75-72 victory was decided in part by a three-point basket Illinois' Sean Harrington hit. "The one rim had a bunch of spring in it and his shot hit almost under the rim, bent it down and the ball goes up and in with this kind of reverse spin. Funniest shot I'd ever seen."

Guenther was impressed by how courageously those Salukis played and when he was introduced as Illinois' new head coach on April 30, 2003, Weber already anticipated some of the transitional growing pains he'd have to contend with. "In my mental approach at the time, it was mostly going to be about teaching and learning the new motion offense and all of that stuff. I don't know if anyone could ever have looked into the crystal ball and seen the hurt feelings the kids were feeling. Kids usually are pretty resilient. And they adjust. When we moved from Carbondale, for the first two months my girls cried and all that. Then, after a while, they make new friends and move on. But the change was harder for my wife and me. The older you are, the harder it is. We couldn't just go to school and meet new friends. It was more difficult.

"I knew teaching the motion offense would not be easy. And one of Bill's assistant coaches told me, 'If you can get those guys to play man-to-man defense the way you want them to, you're a heck of a coach.' Their staff went through some of that frustration the previous year, but with freshmen it's hard to play defense. And Dee, Deron and James had started as freshmen. So I foresaw that. But what I couldn't foresee was the other part of it, the psychological part of it. And the differences in the way we condition and do our individual workouts. Everything was a struggle."

The coaching change was roughest on Dee Brown, who was in tears at the first press gathering after Self's departure. By no coincidence, he was the most difficult player for Weber to win over. And that was significant, since Brown was viewed by the public as the team's charismatic leader.

Weber's approach to physical conditioning started some players grumbling immediately. "In the past they'd done this intense, two-week boot camp thing. Where, to me, basketball is a long season. Conditioning is not an overnight thing. The other thing is, basketball is a sport that is all-inclusive. You have to have aerobic conditioning. You have to run a long time. You have to have quickness and strength. Through the years, we've put the conditioning program together and we've tried to account for all of that.

"The long distance running was really tough for some of them. We're not running a marathon or anything, but some of them had never run distances. Part of it is the aerobic conditioning, but it's also the toughness of running a mile in 5:30. Our guards have to run it in five-and-a-half minutes and the bigs need to finish in 5:45 or six minutes. If you don't make your times, Friday is a penalty day and you run again. And we also run three miles and that's not easy if you've never done it. The long distance stuff just blew their mind."

No one reacted more strongly than Brown. "Dee really struggled with the distance stuff at first. One, he resisted it, so you're starting with a negative attitude. And he'd never really done it." The first to embrace it was Luther Head, probably because it came so easily to him. "Luther, he has no problem going a mile in about five minutes. He probably doesn't even know what he's doing. If someone ever worked with him, he could probably be a track star."

Weber was off recruiting when the negative feedback came flooding in. "I'd get calls every day from the coaches. "They'd say, 'This guy hates it, he's leaving. Dee doesn't want to run.' Every day was a challenge. It was a different guy every day, always someone resisting, someone rebelling. Finally I came off the road one day just to meet with them. I told them to sit down at halfcourt at the practice facility. We have all these championship banners hanging from the rafters. I said, 'Nick, you're a pretty smart guy. How many championships did Illinois win from 1984 to 1998?' Nick said, 'That's easy, coach, there's zero.' And that's right. There's a big hole in there. Then I said, 'How many championships did Purdue win from 1984 to 1998? Well, it's six. You guys probably know some of the history of Illinois basketball. You know there we some pretty good players who came through here, guys like Nick Anderson and Kendall Gill. But other than Glenn Robinson, name a Purdue player?'"

One of the Illini players mentioned Brian Cardinal. "Yeah, but you know him because he's Rod's son," Weber said, a reference to the long-time Illini trainer and current director of basketball operations, Rod Cardinal. "So I asked them to name some other guys and they couldn't. I told them that for a 10-year period Purdue had the best record in the Big Ten. We didn't have great players, yet we were able to win. I asked, 'Don't you guys get it? What we do works. I went to SIU and they hadn't won. We won Missouri Valley championships and went to the Sweet 16. It will work here, too. You just have to trust and believe."

Trust, Weber learned, was not an easily traded commodity. One day assistant coach Chris Lowery pleaded with Weber to yell at the players and demand their trust. "I told Chris, 'What can I yell at them that will get their respect? We have to earn it. It will come, but we have to earn it.'"

Where Brown and some others resisted the coaching transition, Deron Williams seemed to both accept it and thrive under it. "It was amazing," Weber said. "In the first individual session I had with

Deron, he just listened. He sucked it in and listened. I don't know why. I think he liked Bill, so that wasn't it. The only thing I can think of is that Deron's high school coach, Tommy Thomas, is close to Rick Majerus. I don't know if Rick called Tommy and said, 'Weber's a good guy,' or the other way around. I've never asked. But something happened where Deron listened and bought in." Weber suspects that Williams could instantly see personal advantages in the motion offense. "There's no doubt he saw the potential in it right away."

When Weber's first Illini season began, they still lacked a team-wide buy-in. Not everyone had embraced the notion of trust. And when a seven-point loss at North Carolina in the ACC/Big Ten Challenge was followed seven days later by an embarrassing 70-51 loss to Providence in Madison Square Garden, fans turned restless, even surly. Weber calls it the low point during his season of transition.

"Our families were sitting behind our bench and there was a group of Illinois fans who were cussing and drunk. It was ugly. It wasn't all the fans, but there was a group of guys. I didn't hear it while the game was on, but everyone else around us did. My girls were crying on the bus. Coach Nottingham's kids were crying. Wayne McClain's wife was huddled back with Wayne and you could just feel it. The thing that makes me so mad is that I didn't want the Providence game. We were coming off North Carolina and the kids had no respect for Providence. We're young, we're immature, we have no leadership, we don't guard anybody. And if you're not ready to play, it really gets accentuated. I could see it coming."

When the team returned to Champaign, countless hard-biting e-mails and letters were waiting for Weber. "The thing is, we'd just gone through the stuff with Luther (and Aaron Spears and Rich McBride) for the burglary. I had no concentration or energy for practice. My whole day was with one person, then another, then to the chancellor's office, then meeting with the police, then talking to the AD, then talking with parents and to the kids. It just sapped you. It was a mess. And practice just sucked."

Weber's secretary, Cindy Butkovich, was trying to screen the most venomous calls and letters. But some slipped through. "There was one - I might even still have it - that started out, 'To the Coach of the Illini Jailbirds.' I'm sitting back and thinking, I didn't recruit these guys. I'm trying to help them. And I'm getting abused. And this was after the other stuff, where people were mad at Bill for leaving and taking it out on me. I was the one who wanted to be here. So I'm thinking, 'Why did I come here?' And in our staff meetings, the assistant coaches were all upset and screaming and yelling, 'Screw them! Coach, you have to say something. You have to stick up for yourself.' And this writer is saying I don't wear a suit, I don't do this or that. It was stuff that doesn't even matter.'"

All of this had been building to a head when Weber was getting dressed before a game December 11, 2003, against Maryland-Eastern Shore. He was thinking about what he'd say in his pre-game talk. For weeks now, reporters had been asking the players about the transition from Self to Weber and the question was becoming old. Weber wanted to put it to rest. To be truthful, he wanted to once and for all move past the Self comparisons and let this be his team, good or bad.

"So I dressed in all black and told the players, 'I'm wearing black today guys because this is it. This is a mock funeral because we're putting this to bed. It's over. We're moving on.'" Weber's plan was to mention it to the media early in his post-game press conference. But during the game, Deron Williams had broken his jaw in a collision with a Maryland-Eastern Shore player and that subject dominated the post-game comments. Eventually, though, Weber explained his black coat, black slacks and black necktie.

"After it was done, I said I did it for the players. I didn't do it as any disrespect for Bill by any means. If anything it was a compliment because the players liked him. And the fans did, too. But I was trying to make a statement to leave it alone. In the long run, it took the attention off the kids and put it on me and that helped defuse the controversy. There's no doubt it helped. And where it helped was, all the positive people came out. The people who write on the Internet and the people who call radio talk shows, out of 10 calls there's one positive one. But all of a sudden I was getting way more positive e-mails and calls. I didn't do it to get love by any means, but that was a byproduct of it. The kids either thought I was nuts or, 'Hey, this guy is for us. He went out on a limb and did something.'"

The byproduct of Williams' broken jaw, which led to three games missed, was that it forced Brown into a more prominent role. And it forced Williams to lose weight, something Weber had clamored for all along. "Dee took the team upon himself. He still hadn't bought in at that point and I'm not sure he bought in then. But he put us on his back and won some games that were important for us. Dee took it upon himself and played really, really well." Brown's play included an inspired 18-point, six-assist performance against No. 11 Missouri that helped Illinois pull out a 71-70 victory that went a long way toward winning uneasy fans back to Weber's corner.

Inch by inch, positive developments were falling into place. Players were buying in, if only a little at a time. Camaraderie was improving. Trust - the most important component of Weber's new universe - was gaining a foothold.

The team's progress that first season wouldn't be realized until an amazing stretch that produced 10 straight Big Ten victories, six of which came on the road. That earned Illinois its first outright Big Ten championship in 52 years. What began in turmoil advanced to the point that fans were outwardly celebrating a team that had grown and matured together, that had accomplished things few Illini teams had.

Now, one year later, Weber's Illini were light years ahead in their maturation. After beating Oakland in the 2004-05 season's third regular-season game, Oakland coach Greg Kampe delivered a glowing review. "We've tried to play the best teams in the country in the pre-season and we do it for a number of reasons," he said. "In our six years we've played a national championship team and a Final Four team. And for a single night, that's the best team I have ever seen. They passed the ball so well. They are so unselfish. Their guard play is so good. Defensively they get after you. I don't see a weakness. Their unselfishness - the way they pass the ball - that's undefendable.

"Bruce Weber, he's a pretty good friend, and he's a hell of a coach.

In this day and age, it's not easy to get a group of kids that talented to play like that. They are not worried about their stats, about their friends telling them to go pro. He has them bought in. Man, that was impressive. I enjoyed watching it. We got our ass kicked, but I enjoyed watching it."

It's the kind of comment that makes a coach like Bruce Weber proud. But he knows looming on the horizon are two games that will severely test Illinois' talent and resolve, two games that will much more clearly define this team's potential. Gonzaga, with big man Ronny Turiaf, is just three days away. And just beyond that waits Wake Forest, the No. 1-ranked team in America.

CHAPTER SIX

PASSING THE WIZARD'S TEST

Bruce Weber's history with legendary coach John Wooden goes beyond owning his book *"My Personal Best,"* beyond an appreciation for the "Wizard of Westwood's" place in college basketball history. It goes beyond an awe-inspiring respect for the 10 national championships he won at UCLA, a feat that still holds the college basketball world spellbound, the way Joe DiMaggio's 56-game hitting streak does in baseball.

So having a chance to bring Illinois to Indianapolis to play Gonzaga in the John R. Wooden Tradition was an honor and a challenge. Four teams would stage a Saturday afternoon doubleheader at Conseco Fieldhouse, with the four head coaches attending a press conference the evening before with the great Wooden himself, now a 94-year-old lesson in grace and gentlemanly manners.

Weber had always sensed a connection with Wooden. For one

thing, Wooden attended Purdue from 1928-1932 and helped the Boilermakers to the 1932 national championship. He was born in Martinsville, Ind., in 1910 and also coached at Indiana State. So his Hoosier roots ran deep, something not lost on Weber, who lived in Indiana for 18 years during his tenure at Purdue. But it was more than that.

"Actually, a good friend of mine - the guy who got me into coaching - was a high school coach in Wisconsin and for years he worked Coach Wooden's camp. His name was Tom Desotel and he actually hired my older brother, Ron, in Milwaukee. When I was in college, Tom was part of this group of coaches who were real successful in Milwaukee. They ran all these camps. I attended the camps when I was little, and I ended up helping them run the camps.

"And Tom knew Coach Wooden pretty well from working his camps. I could go up to him, as I did at the Final Four in Indianapolis, and say, 'Tom Desotel says to say hello,' and Coach Wooden knows his name and would ask about him. It's amazing. He's still so sharp. Back then there was a group called Medalist

Industries, and they had all these clinics like Nike does now. They did these clinics all over and Tom went and did the notes for the clinics. I was maybe a sophomore in college at the time so I got to go with Tom to Louisville and help with the notes and the setup of the clinic. Coach Wooden was there and Denny Crum and a bunch of coaches. And Coach Wooden walks each morning at like six o'clock or something. So I got to walk with him, along with a couple other guys. We were staying at the Marriott and we just basically walked around the parking lot for a half hour or so. But just to be with him and listening, it was amazing." For Weber, it was like an audience with college basketball's high priest.

Weber's affinity for Wooden has always been there. That's why when Weber chooses an inspirational message to post on the team's message board, there's a good chance it's something he has gleaned from one of Wooden's books. "The night before our game with Gonzaga Coach Wooden had a banquet and he does this talk and it's just amazing. For his age, he's reciting poems at the end of his speech. He's just a special person, all the wisdom there. It's almost like going to church, to be honest. He has so much wisdom and knowledge about life. He's seen it and done it."

Wooden's remarks at the end of the weekend would fill Weber with humility and pride, but first the Illini had to take on a Gonzaga team that was 3-0, ranked No. 24 in the country, and featuring big man Ronny Turiaf, who entered the game averaging 31 points and was coming off a 40-point, 11-rebound eruption against Idaho. Weber knew Wooden would be seated courtside; being critiqued by the master is a little daunting in its own right. But this Illinois team already was gaining a reputation as a group that played hard, shared the ball with unusual willingness, and loved to make the extra pass, a team that could mesmerize a crowd with more than just slam dunks. On paper, the matchup sounded like something the old master might appreciate.

"The one thing we talked about before the season began was whether or not we could stop a good big man, and here was Turiaf coming off a monster game. And obviously we did a great job. He turned it over six or seven times. We knew we had him done when he threw the pass into the stands about 10 feet up. Gonzaga ended up being a very good team, but their point guard was young, and he wasn't ready for our pressure. And then, when we started post-trapping and we trapped all the ball screens, they didn't have any sense of what to do.

"That's the game we started putting Roger on the big guy and had James come and trap. I think if you give Roger one responsibility to focus on, we found out he was pretty good. I thought we could get after them pretty good and put them in a bind. The big thing was, could we deal with their zone defense? But we got so many fast break baskets they almost never got back into their zone. And we made some threes and they had to guard us man-to-man.

"The crowd was unbelievable. There were so many of our fans that made the trip, and that was the first time we got a glimpse of how it was going to be. I remember kids coming into the locker room from the warm-ups saying, 'This is like a home game! There's orange everywhere!' We went out there and we had to have 8,000 or more fans."

The fans had plenty to cheer about. Illinois scorched Gonzaga at every turn, building a 31-point halftime lead and eventually stretching that to 38. Weber's strategy against Turiaf was spot-on, limiting the big man to four baskets and 12 points, 19 below his average. In fact, it got so lop-sided Weber said he felt embarrassed.

"We just came at them non-stop. Mark Few, their coach, is a good guy. You start feeling sorry a little bit. The last 10 minutes we got most of our subs in there. Even (walk-on) Fred (Nkemdi) got to play four or five minutes."

No question Illinois passed the Gonzaga test with flying colors. But what about the John Wooden test? Was the maestro impressed? After the game, Wooden offered up a brief but glowing critique, one that still makes Weber smile. "I thought that was one of the finest performances I have seen in a while. Especially the first half." Weber would gladly kiss the ring of John Wooden, the college basketball icon. Just then, though, it felt almost as though Wooden had returned the favor.

THE RISE TO No. 1

Some games arrive pre-circled on the schedule, already tinted red, and the December 1 Assembly Hall showdown with Wake Forest was one of those. It was a matchup sculpted by network television, a natural with Wake Forest's heralded guards of Chris Paul and Justin Gray against Illinois' fantastic guard trio of Deron Williams, Dee Brown and Luther Head. It was Wake Forest's brawny big man Eric Williams banging inside against Roger Powell and James Augustine. And it was the ACC against the Big Ten in a game that would have RPI (Ratings Percentage Index) consequences for months to come.

But before this match-up unfolded, Illini Coach Bruce Weber and his team found themselves rooting hard for Wake Forest. "We were really cheering them on in the Pre-season NIT," Weber said. "They barely beat Arizona, but we wanted them to come here unbeaten and ranked No. 1. As it turned out, it all laid out perfectly."

"It was great because you have the match-up of the terrific guards, you have Williams and his big, old body in the middle and their other guys were good, too. And the kid we thought was good was their little lefty guard off the bench. When I looked at them I knew they had good pieces, but I thought we had pretty good pieces, too. The one thing we thought was that we didn't know how well they guarded. When you watched film, they were a little loose guarding. That's where we were so far ahead of everyone else.

"I told our guys our goal was to be the No. 1 seed (in the NCAA Tournament), which means we have to have a great record in the non-conference because the Big Ten might not have a great RPI. So I felt we had to win all those games early and to do it we had to guard. And I think they bought into that."

Weber recalls the hype for the Wake Forest game building steadily all week, and he remembers the Orange Krush student cheering section standing in line all night to claim the best seats. "The players brought them pizzas after our meeting the night before the game. And we did donuts for them in the morning. One other game later in the year we brought them breakfast burritos. I actually went out there the morning of the game and walked around talking to them. They're amazing what all they do. Not only on the court, but the stuff they do off the court. They told me because of the number of 3-pointers we made, if they collect all the money pledged, they'll get $700,000, and they think they might be able to finish Rod Cardinal's scholarship endowment two years ahead of time." The Orange Krush is endowing a scholarship in the name of the long-time Illini basketball trainer to be given to a student who pursues the field of athletic training. "And they give tons of money to charities and grants. It affects the whole state."

The night was also "Paint the Hall Orange Night," which has become an annual promotion by a local radio station. When it first began, it turned the Assembly Hall into a shockingly orange backdrop of human commitment. But as the last two seasons have verified, a blinding sea of orange has become a routine part of every Assembly Hall experience. Every night, it turns out, is "Paint the Hall Orange Night."

With the Orange Krush psyched to rock the Hall, Weber had a good feeling about the Wake Forest game. And it became clear early that Illinois would deliver a showcase performance on national television, the kind of effort and execution that would have all of college basketball talking by morning.

"It was like a continuation of the Gonzaga game," Weber said. "Some of it was that we were making shots. I remember Roger telling me, 'Coach, I was making shots I haven't made all year.' It was just that magical environment you talk about. You play at a higher level. And then you break the other team's spirit. And there's no doubt we did that in this game. You put a team on the verge at the end of the half (when Illinois led 54-33), but they always have that chance to recover their spirit at halftime. But we came back out and didn't even let them breathe. At about the 10-minute mark we kind of coasted in," winning 91-73 after leading by as many as 31 points. "Up until then we were coming at them and coming at them. And the ironic thing was, up until then Deron was just playing OK. The media was questioning him. Everyone thought he could dominate. We were playing pretty good basketball against pretty good teams, and Deron wasn't playing that tremendous at that point."

Powell made eight of 10 shots to lead the way with 19 points. Luther Head and Dee Brown added 16 each. Illinois was so precise it barely mattered that Williams' minutes were limited due to foul trouble.

With about 10 minutes to go in the game, and fans nearly exhausted from cheering a near-perfect performance, Weber had time to think about what he'd say in the post-game locker room and press conference. He didn't have to think long.

"When I gave them the schedule in the fall I had circled Arkansas and Georgetown and those were going to be two of our next three games. I told them this would be the true test of what you're about. There's no doubt the trip could be a trap. We had beaten Arkansas so easily the year before. But they were a young team then, it was their first road game and they didn't know if they were on foot or horseback. So now, no matter what I say to our guys, they remember how easy it was last year. But Arkansas had athletes and it was a difficult environment and to move up to the No. 1 ranking, I knew we'd have to win a game in a tough place. So that's what I talked about in the post-game."

Could Illinois make the leap from No. 5 to No. 1? That question came up often. And after leading No. 24 Gonzaga by 38 and No. 1 Wake Forest by 31, just how good were these guys? Everyone wondered that, too. In the post-game press conference, Dee Brown offered this answer: "I don't know what to say," said Brown, who scored all of his 16 points in the first half. "We'll leave it at that. After that performance, you tell me. We made a statement that we're pretty good. We're one of the best teams, if not the best, in the Big Ten. Hopefully we'll continue to get better and be one of those teams that makes noise in March."

After destroying Wake Forest, there already was a loud noise building about this Illini team.

CHAPTER EIGHT

THE TRAP TRIP

BRUCE WEBER WITH MARK TUPPER

The line of communication between player and coach can often take interesting paths. Bruce Weber has learned through 26 years of college coaching that the most revealing comments players make often arrive to him from some of the least likely sources.

Weber is smart enough to know that not all players will run to him to share every issue or observation. Sometimes it's easier to talk to an assistant coach, and it was through the assistants that Weber first began hearing that a building media circus following the Illini team was becoming a drain on the players. It's also how players initially voiced displeasure with Weber's conditioning regimens the season before. And, conversely, it's where Weber first heard that players were quietly whispering that they understood the value in his conditioning system. "I finally heard it indirectly, but Dee Brown came in one day and said, 'Now I understand why we run the way we run.' He realized teams were having a hard time keeping up with us.

"When the media thing started to build, they complained to the assistants more than me. And they complained to Al," Weber said, citing trainer Al Martindale. "I use Al all the time. Players always say stuff in the training room. I watched Coach Keady do it with (Purdue trainer) Denny Miller for all those years. They are as much a part of the staff as anyone. In the players' minds, the trainer is in a neutral position, and they'll say stuff to him. Deep down, they know it will get back to me, but they do it anyhow, because they feel more at ease. They're more off-guard.

"Players are really on-guard with me. They may complain to the assistants just so I'll get the message. But with trainers, you almost get the true drift of what's going on. That's why when Lou Henson decided not to recruit Brian Cardinal, I could totally understand that. The trainer's son is different than an assistant coach's son or even the head coach's son. For a trainer's son to play, now the trainer deals with those guys every day on a different basis and you have that emotional tie with your son. I always thought it would have been a horrible position for Rod to be in, very awkward. They sit in that training room and the players are cussing somebody out. Then all of a sudden it's Rod and some player is cussing out his son. That would have been a tough thing. It made total sense when Lou decided not to recruit Brian, and I don't say that because Brian ended up at Purdue. I don't think the average fan understands that."

As the season built and the stakes became so obviously high, Weber would continue to use the long reach of his information gatherers to keep tabs on the psyche of his team. There was much on the line and having an accurate picture of their mood and demeanor was important.

Weber hoped his team's mood was businesslike and serious heading to Little Rock to take on Arkansas. It was the start of a swing that would bring them four games in eight days, three of which would be played away from Assembly Hall. And coming off the exhilarating rout of Wake Forest, Weber was worried about a letdown that might undercut the hoped-for No. 1 ranking before it ever arrived.

But that didn't happen, a development that was making Weber appreciate this team's mental toughness. "My memory of the Arkansas game was of not being sharp, but of just gutting it out in a very, very loud building," Weber said. "It was a good road test. Even though it got loud, we came up with enough plays. I think that's when we started figuring out there were a lot of different guys who could do things for us. It was a put-back by Roger, it was a little turnaround by Nick, it was Luther getting a layup, then Dee hitting a 3. There were so many different weapons. Our balance showed."

Illinois turned aside an athletic Arkansas team 72-60 with Powell getting 19 points and 11 rebounds. Then it was home for a quick 78-59 victory over Chicago State, Illinois' first as the nation's No. 1-ranked team, before climbing back on a jet headed for the nation's capital.

"Georgetown was going to be a different style of play. They're like Northwestern because both coaches came out of the Princeton system. I think if you're going to be good - and this is something you understand as you get older - you want to go into as many different venues and face as many different styles of play as you can. You're looking at the big picture and trying to be ready for the NCAA Tournament. You want anything that can be thrown at you.

"Something I didn't realize is that we became a national team in part because we faced teams from all the major conferences. We hit every part of the country, from Wake Forest to Oregon to Georgetown to Arkansas to Cincinnati to Gonzaga. So when people are formulating their opinions across the country, we're touching everyone. I think that was part of it."

Weber was pleasantly surprised to find a nice contingent of orange-clad Illini fans at the MCI Center the night Illinois played Georgetown. "We struggled for a while in that game. For the first time all season we took some questionable shots. There's always a spot or two when someone takes a bad shot, but against Georgetown we had a series of shots that were questionable. Then all of a sudden we settled down and started moving the basketball and getting into transition. Our defense picked up right after halftime and I thought we took it to them." Perhaps spoiled by the scintillating performances against Gonzaga and Wake Forest, the Georgetown game was when fans began viewing a 15-point victory away from home as somewhat disappointing. "It's hard to play at that magic level every night," Weber said.

On a rainy morning after the Georgetown victory, the team took a whirlwind tour of some Washington, D.C., monuments and got in a quick shootaround and walkthrough on the Washington Wizards' practice floor before flying to Chicago for its annual game at the United Center against unbeaten Oregon.

"It was one of the hardest tickets," Weber recalled. "I still remember people calling me. I was in D.C. and people were asking if they could get tickets. There were none. They sold standing room only. I remember controlling the game. I was hoping to dominate it, but I think the toll of four games in eight days took a little out of us. We'd miss a lay-up, we'd miss a free throw. I didn't think the game was ever in doubt. But I guess as a coach, you're in Chicago, you have recruits there, maybe the extra Illinois people who never come are there and you're hoping for one of those special performances like Gonzaga or Wake." With Luther Head scoring 23 points, an 83-66 victory was plenty good.

It's an exhilarated crowd that exits the United Center and the buzz is building. The record is 9-0, the ranking is No. 1, and already there is speculation about how long Illinois can extend the unbeaten streak. Weber tried to brace fans for an inevitable loss early in the season. "When we lose a game - and I guarantee you we will lose one - I don't want people to go crazy," he said.

Even now, though, Weber himself is thinking his team can run the table through the non-conference portion of the schedule. When he suggests this to his staff, they roll their eyes. But he's become a fan of setting the bar high. So he sets it there.

CHAPTER NINE

VIVA LAS VEGAS

In order to run the table in the non-conference portion of the schedule, Illinois had just two remaining tasks - win the annual Busch Braggin' Rights game against Missouri and sweep the four games it would play as part of the Las Vegas Holiday Classic. In any season, it was a job easier said than done.

Weber worried about Missouri because of his deep respect for the nuances of rivalry games. "Teams get up for you and it doesn't matter what kind of a season they're having," he said at the time. Sure enough, the Border War battle provided Illinois its stiffest test of the year.

Illinois came into this game whipping opponents by an average margin of 22 points. The closest game had been the 12-point victory against Arkansas. In truth, no team had held Illinois' feet to the fire. But after jumping to a 15-point halftime lead against the Tigers, Illinois definitely got to feel the heat. Poor shooting, foul trouble and a second-half surge by Missouri made it close before Illinois prevailed 70-64. "It was good in that we finally had to make some plays that mattered late in the game," Weber said. "We had to make free throws when they counted. We had to execute on in-bounds plays. Until this game, we hadn't had to do that."

Three days prior to the Christmas appetizer with Missouri, Illinois began its Las Vegas action with an Assembly Hall romp over Valparaiso. All five starters were in double figures as Illinois won 93-56, a game that drew a repeated chorus of "ooohs" and "ahhhs" from a crowd that was wowed by a succession of highlight reel plays. And after a brief break for Christmas, Illinois won its second on-campus Las Vegas Classic game, 105-79 over Longwood behind Deron Williams' 23 points.

Then it was time to take the Illini road show to Las Vegas to try and finish off Weber's goal of staying unbeaten into the new year.

"Before the very first game of the season I put on the message board 13-0," Weber said. "One of the coaches said, 'What are you doing?' I said, 'Well, heck.' I'd looked at the schedule and I thought

Gonzaga was going to be in Indy and we'd have fans there, and Wake was going to be at home. I didn't know if we could do it, but I thought, give them the goal. But I'd added up the number of non-conference games wrong. It was 14, not 13. I didn't realize it until around Christmas. Then I went up there before the Longwood game and wrote 13-0 and crossed it out. I said, 'I probably screwed up. We need to be 14-0.'" And to get to 14-0, Illinois would need to beat Northwestern State on December 30 and 22nd-ranked Cincinnati on New Year's Eve.

"The Vegas trip was amazing," Weber said. "It was like the orange had invaded Las Vegas. People wanted to have good seats in that little high school gym. So for a 6 o'clock game they started getting to the gym at like 11 in the morning, during other people's shootarounds. Other coaches were joking with me about it. I think it was Bob Huggins (the Cincinnati coach) who said, 'You're fans are here at our shootaround. What the hell is this?' But people were watching three games that day just so they could be sure to have a seat down toward our bench. Northwestern State was actually a pretty good team and our kids had to battle them." Illinois did, winning 69-51 behind Head's 18 points, and 12 points and 10 rebounds by James Augustine.

"I think deep down the kids were looking forward to Cincinnati," Weber said. And who could blame them? Not only would one more victory accomplish the 14-0 goal that Weber set for them, but the Cincinnati game was a rematch of the startling 92-68 victory Illinois had posted in the NCAA Tournament the season before. That was a game that gave fans a preview of what this season's team could be like, and it was a stinging loss for Huggins and the Bearcats.

"All the motivation was on their side, and it was a great environment. We're in that small gym banging with Cincinnati's big bodies. It just seemed like a brutal war. We thought the key would be the battle in the paint, dealing with their physical play and rebounding. And we just D'ed them up," Weber said, referring to Illinois' defensive intensity. "We didn't let them get anything. They really had to struggle to score. Cincinnati played tough defense, too, and we didn't score freely. But we still won by 20."

Sure enough, the convincing 67-45 victory cemented Illinois' stature as the No. 1 team in college basketball heading into a new year. And when the game ended, it was time to celebrate in a city that loves to party. On this night, though, Las Vegas nearly outdid itself.

It was billed as the biggest blowout Las Vegas had ever seen, and the normal New Year's Eve hoopla was cranked up to full volume in conjunction with the city's 100th birthday celebration. The Strip was shut down to vehicle traffic. Fireworks were launched at midnight from the roofs of 10 casinos and resorts. People flooded into the streets, and Bruce Weber, his family, the coaching staff and players would soon find out even the best-planned parties can get out of hand.

"That was the craziest place I've ever seen," Weber said. "I was with Megan and the girls and we went to dinner and then wanted to walk around. But there was so much craziness. So we went back to our hotel and you can see where riots start. We got stuck in this glob of people and they were pushing and shoving. My family was scared. We're just in line trying to get to the elevator and one of the shows let out, so there was one group going one direction and another group going the other way and everyone just hit in one spot.

You can see where panic hits people. Some lady pushed my wife. It was crazy.

"Coach Nottingham and his wife had taken their kids to a magic show. On the way back to the hotel, he said he saw five or six guys taken down by cops with handcuffs within a few blocks of the hotel. He got back and his daughter was crying. And we let our players go out and Warren Carter and some of the guys were at McDonald's getting some food when some gang thing breaks out. Our managers just hustled them out of there. That could have been bad.

"Between all that, we just decided to stay in our room. Our daughters were disappointed but the best thing was that the fireworks were right outside our window. We were near the top of the (Paris) hotel and we pulled open the curtains and it was just unbelievable. It was right there, like our own TV show, with fireworks filling the sky. The windows were shaking. We watched the whole thing right there, so it ended up all right."

It would have been a perfect moment to reflect on a season that already had become something worthy of a champagne toast and a fireworks display. Number 1-ranked Illinois was unbeaten and had the country talking about an unselfish style people loved to watch. But Weber said that didn't happen. Not yet. "I think later in the year it did, but not then. We were just trying to keep No. 1 for two weeks, then three, then there were all the doubters. Even though we were No. 1, a lot of people in the national media said we shouldn't be there, that this team is better, that team is better. We had to fight that, too. But it added motivation."

With the start of Big Ten conference play looming, Bruce Weber drew closed the hotel room curtains when the Las Vegas fireworks show finally came to an end. But the curtain was about to open on 2005. And for his Fighting Illini basketball team, the best was yet to come.

CHAPTER TEN

CONFERENCE MEANS KEADY

"We're humble and hungry." That's how Roger Powell Jr. described the team's feeling heading into 2005 and the start of Big Ten conference play. No matter how high the ultimate goals - no matter how much players dream about the NCAA Tournament in March and April - winning the Big Ten conference championship will always stand as one of Illinois' most important team goals. And the chance to win consecutive outright Big Ten championships for the first time in 53 years is enough to get the Illini focused on a new set of priorities.

With the team at 14-0, fans are clamoring about the streak. How far can Illinois ride this shooting star before colliding with an obstacle it cannot overcome? Some fans already are circling the January 25 date at Wisconsin, where the Badgers have proven to be nearly unbeatable. Then there's the February 1 showdown in East Lansing, Mich., against Michigan State. Coach Tom Izzo has a talented bunch and the Breslin Center can be an ear-splitting venue.

But Bruce Weber can't afford to look much into the future. One week - at times only a single game - that's the most he'll let his team think about. The old cliché, "one game at a time," is working with this group, and Weber and his players cling to it, climbing the ladder slowly. Ohio State's visit to Assembly Hall gets league play rolling, and once again it's a team with a talented big man Illinois must confront.

"Terence Dials just killed us the last game of the season at their place," Weber said, recalling Dials' 22-point, nine-rebound performance a year ago. "Everyone said the way to beat us was with a good big man and here was another. We had Turiaf and Gonzaga, Eric Williams and Wake Forest, Jason Maxiell and Cincinnati and now Dials. We struggled in the first half but made some adjustments at halftime and kind of controlled it. Dials got some early fouls and never got into the swing of it." Illinois held Dials without a basket in the first half and limited him to six points overall, 10 under his season average. James Augustine dominated with 21 points and 10 rebounds as Illinois won 84-65.

And while a 19-point victory over a talented Ohio State team might normally make a coach giddy, Weber didn't feel that way with a trip to Purdue waiting next. "We're 15-0, but at the same time we're getting a little stagnant, a little stale. No matter how much you try to prevent it, you're starting to think you're pretty good, and now you have to go on the road in the Big Ten. We went to Little Rock to play Arkansas but that really was a neutral site. And the environment at the Georgetown game was no where near what it is in the Big Ten. So we hadn't experienced anything big away from home yet. I was worried because you have to realize how hard people play at home, especially in the league, and we definitely were not ready."

There was another uneasy feeling building for Bruce Weber, one that he may never shake when the team bus is pointed to West Lafayette, Ind. Having coached at Purdue for 18 years, West Lafayette had been his home and it will always feel a little that way. It's where his daughters were born. It's where he gained credibility as a college coach, thanks to a man who emerged as the most significant male figure in his adult life, Gene Keady. To understand the exceptional circumstances of their relationship, you need only have Weber remind you how they met.

It was a wide-ranging network of basketball coaches that the Weber family came to know in Milwuakee. Bruce's father, Louie, helped run gyms at local recreation centers and, as a people person who never met a conversation he didn't like, Louie Weber got to know just about everyone. That included Bob Gottlieb, who was head coach at the University of Wisconsin-Milwaukee and who happened to recruit Bruce Weber's brother, David. "My dad got to know Bob, and they'd actually go to high school games together and do things together," Bruce Weber said. "My brother ended up going to Bowling Green and transferred back to UW-M and played for him. He's Doug Gottlieb's dad, the guy on ESPN.

"Bob Gottlieb was with Eddie Sutton a long time ago at Creighton. And Coach Keady was with Coach Sutton at Arkansas. So there was a connection. At the time, Coach Keady was head coach at Western Kentucky and his graduate assistant, Jay Williams, left Western in late July to take a full-time assistant coaching position at Wisconsin-Milwaukee with Bob. When I heard that, I had a whim. I wanted to be a college coach. I had graduated from UW-M and had taught fifth grade for one year. At the time I was helping out as a volunteer coach, first at Milwaukee Madison High School and then at Marquette University High School. I had just met Megan but we weren't married yet.

"I had applied to every grad school in the country. I was so naïve. I saw those ads that said, 'Become a grad assistant,' and I just thought that's what I'd do, get my masters degree and become a college coach. I thought it would be so easy and, actually, it did work out for me. But I had applied at Western Kentucky and was accepted into their grad school. Now it's late July and to be a grad assistant for basketball you have to be in grad school and teach a couple classes. So I called Bob Gottlieb and asked him if he knew Coach Keady. He said, 'Yeah, he's an Eddie Sutton guy, I'll call him.'

"So Bob arranged a phone call and I set up an interview to go down to Bowling Green. It's a nine-hour drive from Milwaukee and my older brother, Ron, drove with me. While we're coming down, somebody had called Gene and this guy from Wendy's had a private plane and he asked if they wanted to shoot down to the Pan-American Games which I think were in Puerto Rico. So they took off. It was just one of those things. I had sent my resume, it was a last-minute deal. When I talked to Coach Keady, he said, 'Come on

BRUCE WEBER WITH MARK TUPPER

down, I want to meet you, I want to talk with you.' So I drove all the way down there, I'm scared, I'm a young guy, I'm all excited. And I go to the office and the secretary says, 'Sorry, he's not here.' I said, 'He's got to be here.' And she said, 'Nope, he's out of town and won't be back for a couple of days.'"

Weber was crushed. And because he'd begged for two days off from his duties helping a group of successful Milwaukee coaches run their summer camp, and because he was nearly broke from trying to squeeze a living out of one year as a fifth-grade teacher, he had no choice but to head home. "We just got in the car and drove nine hours the other way."

Weber waited nervously for the day Coach Keady was expected to return to Bowling Green, then stepped from the gym at Marquette University High and poured coins into the pay phone. "I still remember it well. I called him up and he wanted me to come back down. I said, 'Coach, I don't think I can. I have camps. I have to do all this stuff and I just can't take off again. If you want to hire me, you'll have to do it now.' And basically he said, 'OK, I'll hire you. You can have the job.' I was happy, but I think I had Bob

Gottlieb call him again just to make sure I had the job."

Bruce Weber says there's no question that phone call changed his life. But it was only the beginning of an incredible saga that started his life-long relationship with Gene Keady.

"So I got hooked up with the master's program and I had to get a room in the dorm and all that. We took two cars and packed them full of my stuff. My mom and dad drove me down, just like taking a kid off to college. My brother, David, came along and so did Megan, just to see what it looked like. We stayed in a motel and at three or four that morning, the phone rang and it was my older sister, Jan. It was like a nightmare. She said my sister had been killed in a car accident in Milwaukee. She was 13 months younger than me, Carrie, a Christmas baby. She was a senior at UW-M and she was working as a waitress. A Marquette University basketball player, a big guy about 6-foot-9, had picked her up at the end of work and was taking her to our house. And some guy was driving a big pickup truck, going about 45 or 50 miles an hour down a side street. He was chasing a fire truck and he just broadsided them on my sister's side. They said the only reason the basketball player survived was because of his size. He could withstand the blow.

"So my mom and dad go back. I have to stay because I still haven't met Coach Keady. So the next morning I walk into Coach's office and say, 'Glad to meet you. I have to leave. My sister just got killed.' And now I have to go back for the funeral. It was pretty traumatic for my whole family. And while I was home for the funeral, I broke out in hives. I guess it was a reaction from the stress. So now I go back to Western and Coach Keady still hasn't really talked to me. There's a team meeting and I go in there with red blotches all over me. Coach Keady doesn't even know me, and it's just the craziest beginning you could imagine. Clem Haskins was on the staff, and a guy named Ray Hite who played at North Carolina with Phil Ford when they went four corners. And Roger Snapp. And they were all so good to me. That's what Kevin Stallings (another former Keady assistant who is head coach at Vanderbilt) and I always laugh about. I start out like that and end up staying with Coach for 19 years, the longest tenure of any coach ever.

"The thing that amazed me more than anything was, I had pretty good basketball knowledge and Coach actually listened to me. And it got to the point where those guys would say, 'You tell him.' I'm the graduate assistant and they're saying, 'You tell him. He'll listen to you.' And we had a good team and went to the NCAA Tournament."

Good enough so that Keady was able to parlay his success at Western Kentucky into the head coaching job at Purdue the very next year. And even though young Bruce Weber was no more than a first-year graduate assistant, Keady had developed enough respect for him to offer him a full-time spot on his first Purdue staff. "I was so grateful he asked me," Weber said. "To be in the Big Ten, that was great. And I ended up doubling my salary. I made $2,000 at Western Kentucky. That was $200 a month for 10 months. When I got to Purdue that first year I made $3,600, plus a little extra for doing camps. I think it came to a little over $4,000."

Just thinking about their relationship and how it ended up launching Weber's own head coaching career fills him with gratitude. No wonder Weber is overflowing with admiration and respect for Gene Keady, who, ironically, is in his final season as Purdue's head coach when Illinois arrives there January 8 for its second Big Ten game.

"Everything clicked for Purdue early and we were on our heels," Weber said. "You're at the point where you think you're going to win every game and you can lose track of how hard it is." That helped explain the fact that Illinois trailed by nine points in the first half and, for the first time all season, trailed in the second half. But with a large contingent of orange-clad Illini fans making a racket inside Mackey Arena, Dee Brown triggered the comeback. "That game started the tradition where if we got down, Dee was the one - whether it was this game or the Michigan game - he seemed to make a lot of plays. Dee made that hustle play in the first half where he dove out of bounds, saved the ball back in to James, James got it to Deron and he threw it to Luther for a dunk. When you watch it, Dee was like Superman, parallel to the floor. It's kind of amazing, I guess. And Dee made some big threes in the second half and Deron made some nice passes and (Purdue) just couldn't stay with it." The result, a 68-59 victory, provided a bit of a scare. But it was not near-ly as scary as what would come three games later.

CHAPTER ELEVEN

THE IOWA SCARE

Even in early and mid-January, it seemed like every game brought Weber's Illini within reach of another milestone. The victories were growing and so was the historical significance of it all. A victory January 12 at home against Penn State pushed Illinois' record to 17-0, equaling the 1989 Flyin' Illini's mark as the best start in school history. It also marked the 1,500th victory in school history. And just to make sure the historians had plenty to keep track of, Illinois rained in a school-record 15 threes en route to a 90-64 romp.

The school record for the best start ever required a victory at Northwestern on January 15. It was Roger Powell, Jr.'s birthday, but it was Luther Head who blew out the Wildcats' candles with 26 points. Illinois rolled 78-66 in front of 8,117 fans, about half of whom were decked out in orange. Nick Smith scored eight points in the first half to help launch victory No. 18.

When speculating about a potential Illini loss, prognosticators always pointed to a road game. At Wisconsin. At Michigan State. At Michigan. At Ohio State. Never, ever did anyone imagine Illinois could be defeated at home. But while the fans may not have worried, Bruce Weber did. He figures that's just part of his job.

"Coaches are always more on edge than players, whether you coach little kids or older kids. One of my daughters was on a soccer team. They hadn't won a game in a couple of years. But she always thought they'd win the next one. They hadn't even scored a goal. I said, 'You have to score a goal first before you can win a game.' But they're always thinking the best. That's our job, to worry for our kids. That's just part of your job as a parent, a teacher or a coach, to put in that extra worry while they just let it bump off them and move on to the next thing."

When Iowa came into Assembly Hall on January 20, Weber felt he had plenty to worry about. Iowa had not played its best, but he thought the Hawkeyes had one of the best players in the league in Pierre Pierce, and he could see the potential was there for trouble. And it was.

Illinois held a 13-point lead early in the second half, but Deron Williams and Dee Brown were in foul trouble. And Illinois' normally reliable shooting touch went stone cold. For the game Illinois shot 32.8 percent while making just 6 of 28 from 3-point range. Only Head seemed locked in, and as Iowa roared back and tied the game 65-65 with 3.8 seconds to go, Weber knew even he would have to reach a little deeper.

"It was a funny game. It's such a big game for the state. And yet our guys - I don't know if we ran out of emotion or what, or if we needed a jump start again. But, gosh, they were blah. The only one who had it was Luther. That was his best game. He basically was the only one with life. Dee put it on himself in the Purdue game and the Michigan game. Roger did it in the Louisville game. James and Deron had theirs. Different guys, different games. But in that game, Luther took it upon himself. It was almost like his coming out party. He was really good. And so was Pierce for them."

The critical moment came when Weber drew up a play for Head late in the overtime period. "We did a play where we had three screens, and Luther was one of the screeners and he came off another

Louis and Dawn Weber

The Weber children: (clockwise from bottom left) Carrie, Jan, Bruce, Ron, David

Photo Courtesy of the Weber Family

David, Bruce and Ron pose in their bedroom that served as a shrine to their favorite sports teams.

Photo Courtesy of the Weber Family

The Weber men pose on Bruce's wedding day in the alley behind the family home where they first learned the game of basketball.

50ᶜ

Purdue
VS.
Colorado State
November 29, 1980 • Mackey Arena

Photo Courtesy of Purdue Sports Information

Gene Keady and his staff, (l-r) Clarence Grove, Jay Williams and a young Bruce Weber, are featured on the program cover prior to Keady's first game as Purdue head coach.

Coach Weber addresses the media after being named the 16th Fighting Illini men's basketball coach in school history on April 30, 2003.

Coach Weber shakes hands with his mentor, Gene Keady, prior to the Purdue versus Illinois game on March 3, 2005.

Photographer, Mark Jones

The Fighting Illini took in the sites while in Washington, D.C., to play Georgetown.   Here the team poses in front of the Lincoln Memorial.

Photographer, Mark Jones

Legendary comedic actor Bill Murray stopped by and visited the Illini in Chicago prior to the NCAA regionals.

The famed
orange blazer.

Photographer, Mark Jones

Weber looks over his notes for
something that might provide
the Illini with a spark during the
Arizona game.

Photographer, Mark Jones

All-American guards Dee Brown and Deron Williams receive instruction from Coach Weber during the Arizona game.

Coach Weber and his wife, Megan, share a moment after the greatest game in Illini history: Illinois 90, Arizona 89.

As the year wore on it became more and more of a media circus for players and coaches alike.

Photographer, Mark Jones

With all that Illinois accomplished during the season, it's no surprise that Weber swept the 2005 National Coach of the Year awards, claiming the following: the Naismith Award, the most prestigious coaching award in college basketball; the Henry Iba Award, presented by the U.S. Basketball Writers Association; and the Adolph F. Rupp Cupp. Weber was also named National Coach of the Year by the NABC, Associated Press (shown here), *Sporting News, Basketball Times* and *CBS*.

Photographer, Mark Jones

guy's screen. It was kind of a misdirection play where we clear the side. It was a good play, but Luther hit a tough shot from the baseline.

"It was one of those games where you're mad at them because we should have won the game earlier, but they were just not clicking and they just weren't with it. That happens and when it does you have to help them. You have to help them fight through it. You have to coach harder in a game like that. You have to coach every play, I think. Luther didn't want us to lose. And in a game like that, I think sometimes coaches can almost will their guys to win. I've seen it. I've tried to do it. I don't know if it's true or not, but it feels like that sometimes. And that's how it felt that night. It was a close call, no doubt."

Illinois held on, winning 73-68 in overtime. Illinois' poor shooting was offset in part by excellent rebounding. The Illini won the battle of the boards 46-38 with James Augustine grabbing 14. And Jack Ingram, who was becoming an increasingly important factor off the bench, made a difference with eight points and four rebounds.

"It probably was good to get that kind of scare without actually losing," Weber said. "We were getting ready to go to Wisconsin and all of a sudden our guys realized what could happen when we weren't sharp. It turned out to be a good wakeup call."

CHAPTER TWELVE

WINNING AT WISCONSIN

Back in early December, after Illinois had looked so sharp in upending top-ranked Wake Forest, Bruce Weber was on a national TV show when the host said, "Well, you'll go undefeated until the Wisconsin game." The comment surprised Weber because his team was only 5-0 and the Wisconsin game was No. 20 on the schedule.

"I was like, 'Wait a minute! How can you say that?' We're only 5-0. I thought he was crazy." Weber is an interesting mix when it comes to the media. On the one hand, he's a favorite with reporters and commentators because of his brutal honesty and incredible accessibility. He almost never says no to a media request and seems to enjoy the give and take. On the other hand, the Weber family does not subscribe to a newspaper and Weber himself purposely avoids TV and radio shows that include commentary. He'll watch a Sunday afternoon college basketball game, but he goes out to the yard to hit the volleyball with his daughter or switches the channel during halftime when the talking heads chime in with their opinions.

"I used to watch those things, but I can't anymore. They talk about us all the time, and I just get mad. So I stay away from it. When I was at Southern, I'd watch the ESPN shows at night and we were begging. 'Are they going to mention us tonight? Are we going to get a highlight?' Now, I don't like it. I love watching the plays, but when people start talking about other teams, I have to go to the assistants because I don't know names. Unless I recruited them in high school, I don't know their names because I don't watch TV. I just don't."

If there's something Weber needs to be aware of, an assistant coach or Kent Brown or Derrick Burson from the university's sports information department will keep Weber informed. "The only time I see a paper is when I fly. Then I'll get USA Today because it's neutral. We get the papers in our office but the problem is, every time someone tells me, 'You should see what he wrote,' I get mad anyway. So I try not to pay attention."

The exception is when someone's viewpoint might work to Illinois' advantage. Then Weber jumps on it and uses it as a team motivator. That was the case heading into the January 25 game at 18th-ranked Wisconsin. A number of commentators and columnists had suggested that this was the game where Illinois' winning streak would grind to a halt. And it was not an opinion without reason. Wisconsin, after all, had won 38 games in a row at the Kohl Center, the nation's longest home-court winning streak. Illinois had never won in Madison against Badger coach Bo Ryan. And the Badgers had defeated Illinois two of three the season before.

"It probably wasn't true, but it seemed like everyone was picking us to lose. And when Dick Vitale showed up, our kids took it as an insult that he was there to see us lose. I joked all year, any time there was a negative, whether it was Digger Phelps or Dick or Billy Packer, I don't watch it, but the guys do and I just play off of it. Any motivational thing I could use, I try to use.

"But no one had won there in years, so you could see what they were thinking. Actually, you have to give Bo Ryan a lot of credit.

You lose Devin Harris and obviously they're still very competitive. They end up making it all the way to the Elite Eight. He did a tremendous job with them. I don't think we realized how good they were at that point. And you forget how loose and free people play at home."

In game-planning for the Badgers, the Illini coaching staff noted early how different Wisconsin was without the gifted guard Harris. And they changed their strategy guarding Wisconsin's all-Big Ten big man, Mike Wilkinson.

"The more times you play them the more you learn about their system. The first time we played them the year before, when the ball went into the post, Wilkinson was out on the floor. Your first inclination as a big guy is to suck back in. That's what you teach. Well, they do their offense inside-out. Their point guard is inside and he's putting the ball out from the inside. Instead of being a point at the top of the key, he gets the ball off a back screen on the post. Now, those guys rarely score, but what they do is suck everyone down and he pitches the ball out.

"We had a rule, the Wilkinson Rule, which totally defies our defensive rules. When the ball goes into the post, we go touch him. If you remember the game when we lost up there the year before, Wilkinson was just sitting there and our guys are five, six feet away and he gets into a rhythm. Wisconsin played on all of our natural defensive tendencies, the habits we teach. So now, through drills, it's totally opposite. The ball goes to Wilkinson, you go touch him and find him. And he's so clever at slicing for a rebound on a missed shot, when we're making contact with him we're in a better position to keep him off the boards."

Weber credits the scouting reports of his assistant coaches and the film work of Gary Nottingham for finding nuances Illinois might exploit. "Gary's job is to break down every possession and categorize it. He'll give me a tape with every basket they have scored in the last four games. All of a sudden you start seeing tendencies. This is an old Bob Knight thing, but if you can do one or two things to disrupt a team's rhythm or flow as an offense, you've got them. It doesn't take a lot, unless a team is so much better than you."

Illinois' defensive work helped hold Wilkinson to 13 points and five rebounds, only one rebound on the offensive glass. Yet still it was a dogfight as the Badgers battled to continue their home court dominance. Wisconsin was up by eight in the second half, but Illinois mounted a courageous charge. A pair of 3-pointers by Jack Ingram stood out, but Illinois also got 18 points from Luther Head and 14 points and eight rebounds from James Augustine.

"I don't know if it was the aura of the game, but in 26 years of coaching, it has to be one of the top 10 or 15 regular-season games I've ever been involved with," Weber said. "It was loud. And the play of the kids. It just seemed like both teams were playing at a high level. I wasn't sure we'd win until there was like a minute or a minute-and-a-half left. Then you just kind of realize it and you start feeling good. Almost all year, except in the Carolina game, we controlled the last four minutes of the game if we needed to." Sure enough, Wisconsin did not have a basket in the final 4:31 minutes as Illinois finished with a 27-9 flourish.

The 75-65 victory ended the Kohl Center jinx. "It was not only winning there, but to do it so clean, with good, solid basketball. That's when people started talking about what we might be able to do. That was the most excited our kids were all year. Maybe that and the Missouri game the first year and the Cincinnati game in the NCAA Tournament. When they got to the locker room they were leaping around and going crazy. I think they were just so proud."

CENTENNIAL CELEBRATION

While Bruce Weber tries to avert his eyes from the commentary portion of sports TV, he will take a long look at a good sports movie. And one of his favorites is *A League of Their Own*, the story of the All-American Girls Professional Baseball League and the colorful Rockford Peaches. The league was in existence from 1943 to 1954, and the movie follows the Peaches through a championship season. Near the end of the movie, the script fast-forwards more than 30 years later to Cooperstown, N.Y., and the Baseball Hall of Fame and Museum. Many of the women who played in the league have gathered to attend a reunion sparked by the Hall of Fame's exhibit honoring women in baseball. Moving slower, with more gray hair and a few extra pounds, the women are exhilarated to be together again, viewing old pictures and reliving the memories.

Weber felt like he had walked onto that movie set on the night of Friday, January 28 when he attended a reception for hundreds of former University of Illinois basketball players, coaches, managers and support staff. It was the night before the university's season-long 100th anniversary centennial celebration would come to a rousing climax. There would be an alumni game at Huff Hall, and players would be honored at Assembly Hall when Illinois would put its 20-0 record on the line against Minnesota. During a ceremony following the game, all of the basketball alums would be honored and the 20-man All-Century team would be introduced. It would be a huge, emotion-filled weekend.

The turnout was sensational, thanks in large part to the efforts of Rod Cardinal, who tirelessly coordinated the event. Most of the great names in Illini basketball history had returned to campus, including coaches Lou Henson, Harv Schmidt and Gene Bartow. Kendall Gill, Kenny Battle, Bruce Douglas, Eddie Johnson, Ken Norman, Frank Williams, Nick Weatherspoon, Dave Downey, Don Freeman, Duane "Skip" Thoren, Johnny "Red" Kerr and Gene Vance were among the All-Century players who were in attendance. Weber had been given the honor of phoning All-Century players the summer before, informing them of the good news. It still thrilled him how excited Don Freeman and Skip Thoren had become when they received his call. And now, as Weber made the rounds at the Friday night reception, he was struck by the magnitude of it all.

"The whole reception reminded me of that Hall of Fame scene in *A League of Their Own.* I walked into the Ubben gym and to see those guys going through the line, getting their shirts and itineraries and to see the excitement on their faces. A lot of them were in awe of the building. They'd never been to our practice facility before. It was just great. It kind of gave you chills. I saw Coach Henson. It was the first time I'd seen him since he was sick. I had seen him the previous summer when he came back to town. He called me and asked me to meet him for lunch. He just wanted to congratulate me and to talk about different things. And he wanted to play. He wanted to come back to the Assembly Hall with New Mexico State. We worked it out, but then Coach Henson got sick and retired.

"I brought Dee Brown with me to the reception. When we needed a player to do something like that, it was usually Dee, Jack Ingram or Roger Powell. It made an impression on him, too. The night before a game we usually show a scouting report tape. But they'd done this video they were going to show after the game, a highlight tape from Illini history, and we showed that instead. That really hit me. Not tears, but it was emotional. And the players were very quiet. You could tell it meant something to them. We talked a lot about playing well in front of all these former players and coaches, about putting on a great performance. To be honest, there was some pressure on us because Minnesota was a pretty good team."

When game time finally arrived, Illinois was up for the challenge. With the former coaches and All-Century players seated courtside, Illinois took care of business, turning back the Golden Gophers 89-66. Weber could breathe a sigh of relief that his team had avoided putting a major damper on the weekend. To him, though, the reunion was more than exciting. It was an important step that will always have a home in his program.

"There's no doubt you want to keep former players in touch, to make them feel welcome. When you establish a program, like when Dean Smith was at North Carolina, those guys would come back and play with the current players in the summer. Can you imagine going on a recruiting visit and Michael Jordan, James Worthy and Sam Perkins, they're all playing?

"You hope you can get them to come around. Players are funny. I've done it at Purdue and at SIU. Basketball players have been so pampered and spoiled. And sometimes the administration feels the kids owe them something. But you still have to treat them well. And pamper them. And you hope, somewhere down the line, if they are successful and you keep pampering them, it will click in and then it will pay off and they might donate or something. But it's funny, most of the time the guys who are the most giving are not the guys who were the most recruited. They just appreciate it more."

At the end of the All-Century introductions, the formal ceremony came to an end. Basketball alums milled all over the Assembly Hall floor, not ready to leave. Gene Vance, the former Whiz Kid who still resides in Champaign, walked toward Deron Williams and extended his hand. "Keep it going," Vance told Williams, his face deadly serious, the bond from former player to current player showing with crystal clarity. "We will," Williams promised.

CHAPTER FOURTEEN

NEAR PERFECTION

Besides Gene Keady, there may be no coach in the Big Ten Conference who commands Bruce Weber's respect as much at Tom Izzo of Michigan State. That Izzo is the only active Big Ten coach to own a national championship is just one reason Weber thinks so highly of the Spartan's head man. There's also a very solid friendship involved, something that dates back to their days as young assistant coaches who crossed paths on the recruiting trail. Weber was out hustling on behalf of Keady at Purdue while Izzo was doing the same for Jud Heathcote at Michigan State.

If there's one Big Ten coach Weber is most likely to speak with in the course of a typical week during basketball season, it's Izzo, although that could change this year now that Weber's protégé, Matt Painter, slides into the head coach's office at Purdue. But Weber's high opinion for Izzo is deep and sincere.

Competing against an Izzo-coached team is never easy. The

Spartans play hard, play defense, rebound like it's their birthright and love to fly up and down the floor. Izzo has also cultivated a terrific fan following, and his student cheering section, "The Izzone," is a lively and knowledgeable group. Winning at Wisconsin was a major accomplishment, but winning at Michigan State on February 1 would be nothing less. As Illinois arrives at the Breslin Center, Weber knows the Spartans' home court record since the 1998-99 season is a sparkling 102-6. Ranked 10th in the country, Michigan State has enough talent to reach the Final Four, and two months from now that's exactly where the Spartans would find themselves.

By now it's a full-blown media circus following the unbeaten, top-ranked Illini. To accommodate an overflow media throng for this game, the Michigan State sports information office has reporters sitting at makeshift work stations in the Breslin Center hallways. Many reporters stand throughout the game because seating has been exhausted. And, for the first time ever, the post-game press conference will be moved to an alternate room, one large enough to handle the throng here to see if Illinois can rise to the occasion once again.

Illinois' performance is beyond Weber's wildest dreams. In his mind, the Illini play a near-perfect game, the best road performance of the season, better even than the effort given at Madison just a week earlier. Illinois made 13 of 24 three-pointers, got 54 points from its starting guards and shoved past Michigan State 81-68.

"When you think about it, to do that on the road, in a place that has to be in the top 10 in the country as far as winning percentage over the last 10 years, and to do it against a team that would be in the Final Four, and to just control the game, well…. Gary Nottingham keeps the possession chart and during the game I always say to Gary, 'How are we doing?' And he turned to me and said, 'Well, we've scored nine possessions in row.' I couldn't believe it. So I said, 'Well, I guess we're doing pretty good, huh?'" Beginning with back-to-back 3-pointers by Luther Head, Illinois actually made 11 consecutive shots over a period of 12:34 minutes, an accomplishment that certainly made an impression on a sellout crowd of 14,759.

"We played great offensively, but we played well on defense, too," Weber said. "And every time the crowd got loud we shut them up. And the neatest thing was, their crowd is very opinionated before the game. I'm not being negative because their fans are good. But they get after you pretty good before the game. What impressed our players was that after the game was over, their fans were appreciative. Our players were saying, 'You were the one cussing me before the game, and now you want your picture taken with me.' The compliments we received were something.

"The same kind of thing happened after the Wisconsin game. I still remember, we won and Jack Ingram started using his hands to do the 'raise the roof" thing and all that. I told him, 'Chill. I don't want any problems,' and all of a sudden their fans started cheering. I know they were cheering for Wisconsin and also for the streak, but I also think they were cheering because it was a good basketball game. I have to believe that. They were saying, 'Hey, if the streak is going to end, at least someone came in here and played really well to do it.' It was a funny thing. That was one of the most rewarding things all season, the way the fans responded at both Wisconsin and Michigan State."

Now 22-0 and having won at both Wisconsin and Michigan State, Illinois had just eight games remaining in the regular season. Weber was intent on keeping the team's "one game at a time" focus, but even he had to know running the table was now a possibility. Publicly, though, he kept his sights on winning the team's second consecutive Big Ten title. "This one was huge for the Big Ten race because it put us up by two games on everyone, and Michigan State couldn't get it back because they didn't play at our place. I knew we were in control."

But now, even Weber admits the thought of shooting for 30-0 had crept into his mind. "I never brought it up to the players, but, yeah, I started to think about it. I didn't even talk about it with the coaches. But you definitely started thinking about it. I just thought, 'We can do this. We can get through this thing.' I knew the end stretch was not going to be easy. We still had to play at Michigan and all along we feared Ohio State. We knew they were on (self-imposed) probation, and we knew what a big game that would be for them. But after beating Michigan State, yes, I knew it was something we might be able to do."

After the victory, the team flooded back into a happy locker room. But Weber noticed a different reaction than the all-out celebration he'd witnessed in Madison. "They were excited, but it wasn't as emotional as winning at Wisconsin. They felt good about it, but they were a little more subdued." By now, winning on the road - something Illinois had done 10 straight times dating back to the 2003-04 season - had become this team's calling card.

CHAPTER FIFTEEN

STRINGING THEM TOGETHER

"Maybe Illinois can't lose."

After the two impressive road victories, that had become college basketball's hot topic. Bruce Weber and his Illini were everywhere - TV, radio, newspapers, magazines - and they had splashed on the national scene as the hottest thing since Air Jordans. Even a brief media blackout, imposed by Weber prior to the Wisconsin game, couldn't slow an all-out rush to tell the world more about this likable team and its raspy-voiced coach.

OK, the voice. When Weber speaks, it's as though something sharp and jagged has lodged in his throat. It's as though he has gargled with razor blades or sipped from a bag of wet sand. Raspy, gravelly, at times a little squeaky, Weber's voice is the result of childhood surgery to burn polyps off his vocal chords. "I was probably eight or nine years old and I'd always had a lot of throat and ear infections. I went to the ear, nose and throat guy all the time. I'd take a bus to downtown Milwaukee with my mom. They finally decided to do something, so they removed my tonsils and lasered the polyps off my vocal chords.

"I remember one day sitting at breakfast after the surgery, and the doctor said, 'You really have to stop yelling. You strain your voice.' Well, our house was loud. We had five kids, a dog, and friends were over all the time. My dad had a hearing aid from an accident in the military and when we came home you had to yell like crazy to get his attention. My mom kept on me about it, saying, 'You have to watch your yelling.' The doctor suggested I never go into any profession where I had to yell a lot. And that became a joke because I was the loudest person and yelled the most.

"I'm not kidding when I say our house was loud. There would be a game going, the TV was on, the stereo was on, there were always people visiting, the dog was barking and dad would come home and take the hearing aid out and go hide. It was a very loud house. When I first took Megan there, she couldn't believe how loud it was but that was just kind of accepted there. It's how it was."

So since he was a kid, Weber and his raspy voice have been pushing the limits of his vocal chords. If nothing else, it's distinctive and it seems to play well on radio and TV, where his self-effacing jokes routinely draw giggles and laughter. Knowing the exposure was good for his program, Weber fielded more media requests than he could ever count during the course of the season. On the one hand it was a blessing for a man who admitted much of the country was still learning to recognize his face. But it was a burden as well, primarily for the players who found the constant attention a bit overwhelming, and at times for Weber, too, who was his own worst enemy because he couldn't say no.

"The crazy thing is, whenever I had to do a live thing with TV, I had to go to the local TV studio and I can't even see the people I'm talking to. I hate those. I'd do I-Max or Jim Rome or Best Damn Sports Show or ESPN or ESPN Cold Pizza, all of them. And they're talking to me and laughing and making fun of me, but I can't see them. So you smile and just kind of take it.

"The one everyone remembers was with Steve Lavin on ESPN. I'm talking to those guys one night, and Steve was making fun of my orange shirt and orange ties and then someone says, 'Well, he's making fun of you, what can you say about him?' Well, I can't see him, but I say, 'I didn't know Steve was going to be making such a fashion statement.' I was talking about his hair, which he greased back. But what I didn't know was that he had changed his hair style and that's what they thought I was talking about. I never even saw it and I'm in the car later and people are calling me and going nuts. "You got Lavin about his hair! That was hysterical!'

"But the line everyone remembers was when Lavin was making fun of my orange clothes. I said, 'Once you go orange you never go back.' To be honest, I thought of that a long time ago. I was going to say it one time at an Orange Krush thing but never said it. I had that bright orange shirt on and for some reason it just came out.' Then Lavin said, 'Do you even have orange undies?' I said, 'Not yet,' but the next day four pair of orange underwear were brought to the office. And one of them had been embroidered."

The media requests kept stacking up, and Weber scrambled to field them all. "It really did get to be a circus after a while. At first Kent (Brown, the sports information director) said, 'We have to strike while we're hot. We can't turn this down. We can't turn that down.' But it did start to get weary. And finally, once when I was out recruiting, I called Kent at one or two in the morning ("I leave a lot of messages late at night when I think of things") and said, 'After tomorrow we're done and we're closing it off. You can say what you want, but we have to give the guys a break.' And the players were so happy. I didn't even tell them about it. We came in and went through practice, and I said, 'Did you guys notice anything different today?' And they said, 'Yeah, where are all the media?' I said, 'They're not here. They're out.' And they started giving me high fives. They just needed a little break from it.

"At first it was just our regular beat guys and our weekly thing we do with them on Mondays. They're used to that. But then *USA Today* came and then it went to ESPN doing a special and Fox doing a special, and we had that film crew in doing that piece for Nike. And then the Chicago stations were practically living there. And then it was the *New York Times* and *Sports Illustrated*. Well, Dee kind of thrives on it, and Deron does all right. But Luther, he's the one it took a toll on.

It's mentally draining for him. He wants to do well and he really

tries, but it's hard for him. And now it goes from maybe three min-

utes with our beat writers to a 20-minute thing with *USA Today* to

30 minutes with *Sports Illustrated* and it just took a toll."

Weber, though weary, never stopped. At midnight on a Sunday, he

could be heard talking to former Georgetown coach John Thompson

on his syndicated radio show. Or one might catch Weber's familiar

voice jabbering away on a tiny radio station in downstate Salem. "I

don't know if I ever said no to anyone. Kent and those guys might

have weeded some out, but a lot of people went around those guys.

If they know me, they just call my cell phone. Dave Kaplan from

WGN just calls me. He doesn't even mess with them. He knows if

he calls me I'm not going to say no. If he goes through them he

might get put off a week or so. Andy Katz (from ESPN.com) just

calls me."

"Some guys get mad because they'll say Kent told them I wouldn't

go on the air with them, but they heard me on some podunk station

somewhere. But maybe I knew the guy from Southern. Or he was a

former team manager or a guy who did free stuff for us at SIU. I just have a hard time saying no to them."

After the victories at Wisconsin and Michigan State, the national college basketball attention was aimed squarely at the Illini. A victory at home against Indiana followed. Then came a scare at Michigan, one averted when Dee Brown all but assured he would be named Big Ten Conference Defensive Player of the Year by making three steals in a game-changing stretch in the second half. Wisconsin came looking for revenge on February 12, but Luther Head scored 26 and Brown nailed a pair of 3-pointers down the stretch that sealed a 70-59 Illini victory. Consecutive road wins at Penn State and Iowa followed, and Illinois was still college basketball's darling, rolling along with a 27-0 mark that kept Weber scurrying back and forth to the local TV studio for more.

CHAPTER SIXTEEN

THE CLINCHER

The message board that Weber uses to help hold his team's focus contained three items when he'd finished his colored-market scribbling. Two dates. One word.

"It was right at the time when I worried we might be losing our focus a little. I could tell and I'd heard some things," Weber said. "We were getting a little ornery, I'd heard they were out celebrating too much and I wanted to talk about it. It was right when we found out the date of the Purdue game, so I wrote that on the board - March 3. Then I also wrote April 4. And I wrote the word, 'Commitment.'

The commitment message was designed to remind players what was at stake, that goals of a lifetime were now within reach. "I told them, 'Physically, mentally, we can't have any distractions. No problems off the court. No one getting into trouble, no jealousies. I

BRUCE WEBER WITH MARK TUPPER

knew they were starting to vote on the post-season awards. And I reminded them about taking care of their bodies. The season wears on you. You have to get your sleep and eat the right foods. The flu was going around. All of us were feeling it. Our team doctor (Dr. Jeff Kyrouac) gave me five or six shots during the season just to keep me going. One time he showed up during practice and told me to drop my pants right in the middle of the gym. I thought he was kidding. But he wasn't, so I did.

"I'd heard our guys were out until three or four in the morning the Saturday after a game. Hey, I don't care if they go out, but you can't wreck your body. When I was young I thought I could do it, but you realize you can't. It takes a toll on your body. So I wrote, 'Commitment.'

"Then I asked them, 'What is March 3rd?' Jack said that was going to be senior night. 'Yes, it's your last home game. Make a commitment to be undefeated at home. Celebrate the seniors and an outright championship.' We actually clinched it before the Purdue game, but we'd made the celebration plans. The year before we clinched on the road, and we didn't get to cut down the nets. I told Rod Cardinal I wanted to have a celebration. I wanted the confetti cannon, the fireworks, I wanted to cut down the nets and I wanted to have a trophy on senior night, the whole thing."

But an already jam-packed night had another twist. This would be Gene Keady's final visit to Assembly Hall and the Purdue head coach had spent much of 2005 reluctantly accepting gifts on his Big Ten farewell tour. Weber, naturally, wanted to do something special for the man to whom he owed so much.

"It turned out to be a circus. That was a lot to do in one night, and you worry about all of those things. And you worry about playing good. But that was when Dee was in his streak, really on a roll. He was unbelievable then. As it turned out, I usually get kind of sad with the senior night thing. Every time I've been involved, even as an assistant, it's kind of emotional. But my mind was going 100 miles an hour, what I was going to say for Coach, what we were giving him. It was overwhelming and it kind of took something away from it for me. And deep down, you have to think it might be

Deron's last home game and, who knows, maybe Dee's last game. And they don't even get honored. So there was a lot going on."

Dee Brown had a lot going on, too. He came out blazing, using the game as his personal stage in the quest to win Big Ten MVP. He scored 24 of his 26 points in the first half as Illinois steamrolled the Boilermakers 84-50. His final points of the first half ignited an explosion, and the team heard an Assembly Hall louder than it had been all season.

"They had a full-length pass with three seconds to go but threw the ball out of bounds, so we got to run one final play. All I did was call a basic, simple sideline thing, and Dee hits this wild three falling down and Deron jumps on top of him, and it's right in front of Coach. And he gets ticked off. I didn't see it but everyone tells me about it. We were beating them but we really put it on them right before the half. I played a lot of subs, even in the first half. Then we come out the first three or four minutes of the second half and just crush them. I'm looking at my coaches saying, 'What do I do?' I'm looking down there at the Purdue bench and seeing long faces, and I don't want to rub it into Coach or Matt Painter. But at the same time it's our seniors' last home game. It wasn't even the first TV timeout in the second half, and I said, 'God, we've got to take them out.'

"In their mind, I think they still felt we rubbed it in a little bit. But by no means did we do that. Coach was fine afterwards. I think Matt calmed him down. I just felt bad about it. At one point I told our guys in the huddle, 'I'm just asking for me. You can kick their butt, I don't care. But do not rub it in or act up. Please.'"

It was a bittersweet victory for Weber, who addressed the crowd with the promise, "We're not done yet," after the game and just before the team cut down the nets to celebrate another outright Big Ten title. It was a moment to acknowledge a great team achievement. But it was difficult for him to watch Keady, the consummate competitor, shuffle away in defeat.

"The man is like a second father to me," Weber said. Indeed, Weber's own father, Louis, died in October of 1986 at age 63.

Weber had been at Purdue for just five years, so if there were times when Weber needed a father figure during his final 13 years with the Boilermakers, chances are it was Keady he turned to. Now, he just wished there was some way to send his mentor off with a smile.

Even Weber's family found winning against Keady to be bittersweet. Daughter Hannah, who already was a student at Purdue, cried when Keady announced he'd be retiring. She'd known him her entire life and, like her dad, the fondness for him ran deep.

CHAPTER SEVENTEEN

FINALLY, A LOSS

There was no eerie vibe, no black cloud, no disturbing vision in the middle of the night that makes a man leap from his mattress in a cold sweat. After polishing off Purdue, one final victory at Ohio State was all that stood between Illinois becoming the first Big Ten Conference team to sweep through the regular season unbeaten since Indiana in 1976. 30-0. It had a perfect ring to it. And all signs pointed toward it happening.

"By then, everyone was talking about finishing it off," Bruce Weber said. "I didn't have any bad feelings going into it. I think the kids wanted it. It wasn't a goal I originally set for them but, once we started talking about it, I know it was something they wanted. We had an article with comments from Quinn Buckner about all the pressure they went through at Indiana, and I focused on that. And they watch TV and people were talking about making history and being in this elite group. So, yes, I think they wanted it."

BRUCE WEBER WITH MARK TUPPER

If there was anything resembling a bad omen, it might have taken place near the hallway that leads from the Value City Arena floor to the Illini locker room. Weber was walking through after the team initially arrived at the Buckeyes' spacious arena when a fan spotted him and shouted, "You're going down today, coach!" Weber never broke stride and in his trademark voice instinctively said, "Thank you," a response that aficionados of his speech patterns love to hear him say.

Ohio State had been in the back of Weber's mind all along. He respected the Buckeyes' talent, thought highly of their coach, Thad Matta, and understood that Ohio State would have a world of motivation in its corner on this Sunday afternoon because there was no post-season reward to look forward to. The Buckeyes had self-imposed a post-season ban due to alleged recruiting violations, and today would be their chance to shine in the national spotlight.

The game started perfectly for the Illini as they zipped to a 16-4 lead. "If anything, we got off to too good of a start," Weber said. "We kind of controlled the game and got lulled to sleep a little bit." Nevertheless, Illinois led 38-27 at the half and was still ahead by 11 when Nick Smith hit a baseline jumper with 10:59 to go. But that's when Ohio State started chipping away, mostly by going to 6-9 Terence Dials, who'd had a sub-par game in Champaign, and by letting 6-7 Matt Sylvester take defenders off the dribble.

"When they started making the comeback, I think we got a little tight. We didn't make plays. We didn't have a good flow. The crowd got into it and it was really loud. We didn't score for the last three or four minutes of the game and even though we couldn't score and you felt it slipping, I still thought, 'Man, we're going to get a stop.' And all season long at least one of our guards stepped up. One game it would be Dee, another game it would be Luther, another game it would be Deron. And most games it was more than just one of them. But this time all of them struggled." Indeed, Illinois' three starting guards made just seven of 27 shots and combined for 27 points, their second-lowest output of the season.

Despite the feeling that the game and the unbeaten regular season were slipping away, Illinois still had a chance if it could muster one final defensive stop on an Ohio State possession that began with 12.1

seconds to play. Illinois was clinging to a 64-62 lead. During a time-out, Matta informed his team that they were going for the win. Over in the Illini huddle, Weber and his staff talked about what needed to happen on defense. Pressure the ball. Fight through screens. Make no errors. Hold nothing back. But in just one of the few times all season, talk did not translate into action.

"Everything we talked about in the huddle, we didn't do. We wanted pressure on the ball, and there was none. I go back and watch the film, and Dee was like 15 feet off of him. But he had four fouls and after the game he came up and apologized. He said, Coach, I'm sorry. I didn't put pressure on the ball. I had four fouls and wanted to be in there in case we went to overtime and needed a play.'"

Dials set a screen for Sylvester, designed by Matta to be the shoot-er, and he swished the game-winning 3-pointer with 5.1 seconds to go. "Deron was on Sylvester and we had talked about switching because a lot of times we switch everything. But I said, 'No way. If they do a down screen, we're going to end up with Dee on Dials, and we can't do that because they're going to Dials.' So instead, they do what we call a single-single into a flare, and Deron doesn't fight through the screen. Mentally he can say he thought someone was going to switch, but…. There was no pressure on the ball, and no one fought through the screen. It was a sad thing."

Amid the frenzied eruption from a crowd of more than 19,000, chaos followed Sylvester's shot. "The crazy thing is, if you go back and watch it, Thad is calling timeout when they hit the bucket. They don't give him the timeout. But the referee at halfcourt turns and sees me and gives me the timeout. Now there's an argument almost the whole time, and we don't have a play in, so I had to take another timeout, our last. If the refs had given Thad the timeout he asked for, we still would have had another one. That ended up being kind of important.

"Then we run a play we have practiced all year. You look for Deron; if he doesn't get the ball James screens and then he pops out and gets it, now Deron is supposed to be running on a diagonal. It didn't work but we got lucky because the ball was deflected out of bounds. That's when we needed the other timeout. But even with no time, the kids reacted well. Without a timeout you just kind of yell it out. We got the ball to Roger, but he rushed it and his shot missed. But he'd never been through that before. He had more time than he realized. He had time to dribble and square up. He was wide open." Weber said if he'd had a timeout, he might have subbed in Jack Ingram, a better 3-point shooter. But with no time-outs remaining, there was only time for the final mad scramble.

For the first time all season Illinois witnessed something they had pledged not to let happen. "We'd talked all year about not letting someone storm the court. And now they're storming the court, yelling at you, all that stuff. It was sad. So I'm starting to get mad, trying to get off the floor. I'm the first one to the locker room because no one else could get through all the people on the floor. I usually let the players go in and talk, and I talk to the coaches. So I go in and kick something, and I'm really mad. Then I thought, 'What the heck am I mad about? We're 29-1 and have a lot ahead of us.' But the players were mad, too. I guess we all were."

An on-going debate had focused on whether a loss would be good or bad for the Illini. Weber would have preferred a perfect game and a runaway victory. But in retrospect, he said the loss did not hurt. "There's no doubt it was good for us. Our guys had to watch film and they had to pay attention. We didn't play great. I'm not sure they deserved to win, but I'm not sure we did, either. It was going to catch up with us.

"The Northwestern and Purdue games had been what I call disillusionment games. Northwestern went through some tough times at the end of the year. Purdue, they were so tired and they had no players. Those games were not real. You're at home and Dee is making threes like crazy. Things are happening that shouldn't happen. Now, you go into a game and it starts out too easy. You get the illusion that it will be that easy, and it's not going to be.

"It brought us back down to earth and gave us a motivation for the Big Ten Tournament. I was dreading the Big Ten Tournament that last week going into the Ohio State game. So you go 30-0. The only hope then is that they love Chicago, they love playing in the

United Center. But was that going to be enough to get past Iowa, who was trying to get into the NCAA Tournament? Was it going to be enough to get past Minnesota, which was fighting for a tournament berth? Was it going to be enough to get past Wisconsin or Michigan State? I'd have rather won the game at Ohio State, but given all that happened, a loss there didn't hurt us. It hurt that day, but it didn't hurt us in the long run."

CHAPTER EIGHTEEN

THE HEARTBREAKING WEEKEND

For the time being, the Big Ten Conference has decided to dribble its men's basketball tournament back and forth between Chicago and Indianapolis. And this season was Chicago's turn to play host, which pleased Bruce Weber if only because it was at the United Center where Illinois won its only Big Ten Tournament championship in 2003, and because it gave his mother, Dawn Weber, shorter travel distance from her home in Wisconsin.

The season had been an amazing experience for the proud mother of the Illini coach. She watched the games on the satellite system her son purchased for her and was amazed at how frequently she saw her boy's familiar face on TV. "It's like a fairy tale," she told him. No doubt she thought about all those years in Milwaukee, when the kids would shoot hoops in the basement, in the parks and at the rec center with her husband, Louie. Her other sons had also become coaches, and she was equally proud of them. Her youngest boy, David, was leading Glenbrook North High School on a storybook trail toward the Illinois High School Association Boys Class AA state championship, and she planned to take in his sectional championship game that weekend, too. Privately, Bruce Weber and his sister, Jan Moeller, a counselor at Joliet Junior College who lived in Frankfort, 35 miles southwest of Chicago, worried that the toll of such a busy weekend might be a bit stressful for their mom.

Meanwhile, though, Weber was busy shifting his team into its post-season mindset, the one-and-done psyche that brings the nation's best teams to full alert. Coming off the only loss of the season, what Weber and the Illini needed now was a nine-game winning streak. Three to clinch the Big Ten Tournament title and lock up a No. 1 seed in the NCAA Tournament. Then six in a row to win the school's first national title. Nine games. Nine victories. After opening the season 29-0, nine more didn't sound impossible.

First up was an 11 a.m. game on Friday, March 11, against Northwestern, which had advanced by eliminating Michigan one day earlier. "Our guys had decided they hated to play early games, but I thought we played pretty good against Northwestern," Weber said. "James was very focused. That's when Dee kind of lost his confidence. I don't know what happened. It just wasn't clicking. But Deron was really stepping up. He obviously was making his run to the NBA. And we played good enough to beat them pretty soundly. It wasn't a masterpiece, but for an 11 a.m. game it was pretty good."

Immediately following the 68-51 victory over the Wildcats, Weber was brought to the post-game interview room, a makeshift area off the media's main work room, cordoned off with dark blue curtains. Weber stepped up onto the stage and answered questions, as he always does. But as the session ended and as he stepped down to begin making his way back through the maze to the Illini locker room, his wife, Megan, was waiting there to greet him. That alone told him something was wrong.

"She never comes to those things. I guess she doesn't think that's her place. And she says, 'I've got to talk to you. Your mom was taken to the hospital. It could be really bad, but maybe not as bad as it sounds. We just don't know.' My mom already had a lot of stuff health-wise, some mini-strokes and things like that. And the funny thing was, I'd talked to my sister on Wednesday, and she said, 'I don't know if mom can make the whole thing. She just gets worn down so fast. For her to travel, go to your game, then go to David's game, that's a lot of excitement.' We just agreed we had to be careful and watch her."

Bruce Weber thought he understood the urgency of his wife's message, so he told her he'd finish answering the media's questions outside the team locker room, as he routinely did, then leave for the hospital. "But she said, 'No. Your mom could be in trouble.' I had no idea."

Dawn Weber made the drive down from Wisconsin with Bruce's niece, Claire, who lived in Milwaukee and had just graduated from Marquette with a degree in journalism. They arrived at the United Center and went directly to the will-call window to pick up the tickets Bruce had left in her name. Dawn Weber began to feel pains in her chest, serious enough to warrant immediate medical attention.

"The United Center people and the Big Ten did a great job. They got her into an ambulance and over to the hospital (Rush University Medical Center) in minutes. Megan didn't know that much about the details. Claire and my sister went with her to the hospital, and mom kept saying, 'Don't tell anybody. We don't want to bother Bruce or David. I'll be fine.' That's just my mom. And Jan didn't want them telling me, either, because they still didn't know how serious it was. In fact, my mom sent my niece back to watch our game, telling her, 'I'm fine.'"

Dawn Weber was not fine. In a short time doctors would determine she had a ruptured aorta, the largest artery of the body that rises from the ventricle of the heart. It's a grave situation for anyone, particularly so for an 81-year-old woman who already had health problems.

Bruce Weber still didn't know how grave her situation was. "I went straight over to Rush and it was kind of funny when I got there. They made a big deal out of us, and I thought maybe it was because of me, Illinois, and they put us in a special room and they were bringing us food and drinks. I was thinking, 'Golly, they're being pretty nice.' But I think they knew my mom was pretty much in trouble." By the time he arrived at Rush, his mother already was in surgery, a procedure they said could last six hours.

"I found out later, when she was going into surgery, the doctor really knew there was a problem. He said, 'Every minute counts,' and my sister said she was running with the cart on the way to surgery. It was a fast break to the surgery room. And my mom told my sister, 'Is my ticket still in my purse? Maybe I'll still get to come.' That was her thought. My mom was always a tough, stubborn lady.

"While she was in surgery we started to get an inkling. Other people started coming around. They started getting phone calls in the room. I could sense something. I didn't have a good feeling about it. Then one doctor came in and said it didn't look good. He said they did the first patch but as soon as they opened it up everything started breaking up. He said she had fought through it, so they were going to keep trying. They had to massage her heart several times to keep it pounding. I said, 'Is there any hope?" He said, 'Very little.' And an hour or so later the surgeon came in and said she had died.

"The bad thing is, it got announced before we really even knew. I don't know how but it did. And it was pretty sad because we didn't even get to call her brothers and sisters. They found out on TV before we did. That was kind of sad. The P.R. guy from the hospital, he came up and met with me. He said, 'We understand your status, we're trying to keep you isolated.' There were media and TV stations in the hospital. He said, 'We're going to do our best, but we want you to read the release, whatever happens.' But the release went out before we knew. I could tell because my cell phone started ringing. You're sitting there the whole time, and there's a time when we thought everything was going to be OK. But then you find out and it hits you. It's hard.

"I never got to see her. They brought her into a room after she had passed and that's when you get to have your final time with her. We went once and then you want to go again. A lot of things run through your mind. I remembered all those times when she was with me at the emergency room, how she always took care of me. So it was really hard losing her."

Phone calls informed the rest of the family, and after Ron Weber and his family arrived from Waupaca, the decision was reached that Bruce would coach the next day against Minnesota. "My mom knew basketball was our life. She loved her kids and she was so proud of us. She wanted us to be successful. We all agreed we had to try and coach."

Later that night, drained and dazed, Bruce Weber returned to the team's Hyatt hotel on Wacker Dr., and when assistant coach Wayne McClain was spotted swooping through the lobby just before midnight, he said Weber had already joined the coaching staff in the team's film room and was helping to prepare for the Golden Gophers. He did not arrive there alone.

"There were some guys with me who came to our house all the time when we lived in Milwaukee," Weber said. "Good friends. We watched some film and reminisced about my mom. I really didn't sleep that night."

The emotional tidal wave would hit in public the next day. "It was hard at first, walking into the United Center and all the media waiting. Then I had to go on TV to do some pre-game stuff. Then some things happened I did not expect. First, Rod Cardinal gave us all black bands to wear on our uniforms. I said, 'How did you do that?' I mean, it had only been a matter of hours. And then he comes with orange and black ribbons for the coaches. Then the Big

Ten office decided to honor mom with a moment of silence before the game. I didn't know anything about it until it happened and it surprised me. That was hard and I kind of broke up for a minute, but it was very special to my family."

Once the game started, Weber said he was able to temporarily push the wave of emotion to the side, concentrating on Minnesota. The Gophers' Dan Monson is one of Weber's close Big Ten coaching friends, and they had embraced before the game. Several of the Minnesota players made a point of seeking out Weber and clutching his arm or shoulder and expressing their sympathy. That the game went on fairly normally amid such an outward expression of grief is rather amazing.

Illinois won the semifinal game 64-56 with all five starters landing in double figures. James Augustine, who would be the MVP of the tournament, had 14 rebounds, and Weber remembers the effort more than the precision with which it happened. "We didn't play great, but we played with a lot of emotion. I think that might have been the highest our play-hard chart was all year. I still remember one moment after the game when James and Deron kind of came up and grabbed me. They're kids and I didn't really think it would have an impact on them. But I think it did."

A standing room only crowd of 23,697, waves of which were wearing orange, showered affectionate applause on Weber from the time he first marched onto the floor until he left with an appreciative wave after completing a post-game television interview.

Before the game, Jack Ingram stood on behalf of the team and let Weber know they were thinking of him and sharing in his grief. Then Weber talked. "I just told them you have no choice in controlling life and death. I had just witnessed it. There we were at Rush Memorial, one of the best cardiac units around, with a surgeon who is renowned in his field, and he couldn't save my mom. The one thing you can control is what you do everyday, and that's your attitude. Basketball games, the NCAA Tournament coming up, in the larger scope of life they may not be that big. But how you approach it is something you can control. It's how you're viewed. Why pout? Why be a grump? You have a great opportunity. Don't worry about some nit-picking selfish thing. You have to deal with life and you have an opportunity to do that now."

The next day Illinois continued that quest, using clamp-down defense to turn aside Wisconsin 54-43 for the Big Ten Tournament championship. The Badgers shot just 25.9 percent and Roger Powell, Jr. led the way with 15 points and 12 rebounds. Less than an hour later Illinois was rewarded with the No. 1 overall seed in the NCAA Tournament and sent to Indianapolis, where its first-round opponent would be Fairleigh-Dickinson.

"There was a lot still going on with my mom's funeral and all, but it was time for us to get focused on the NCAA Tournament," Weber said. "It's what we had been pointing toward all season. And now it was here."

CHAPTER NINETEEN

FIRST STOP, INDY

The funeral was on Tuesday and a private plane was made available for Bruce Weber and his family so they could fly from Champaign to Wisconsin to say goodbye to Dawn Weber. Bruce's brother, David, would attend the funeral and return in time to coach and win his Supersectional game that night. All in all, it was another hectic, nearly frantic, emotion-packed week for the Weber family.

More than ever, perhaps, Bruce Weber was leaning on his coaching staff, confident in their ability to prepare for Fairleigh Dickinson in the first round of the NCAA Tournament and either Texas or Nevada in Round Two. He would help, of course, and stay as involved as he could. But there was no question his focus was split between the desire to properly put his mother to rest and the urge to give all of his attention to his team. The first-round site was the RCA Dome in Indianapolis, and Weber was counting on the Illini fans to take advantage of the friendly regional proximity. They did not disappoint.

Although no No. 16 team has ever defeated a No. 1 seed in the NCAA Tournament, there's always a first time. And no coach wants to be victimized by that first time. "That's always a fear. You're expected to win and when you watched Fairleigh Dickinson on film, I thought physically and athletically they'd have trouble with us, but they did have some skills. And our fear, if you let yourself look ahead, was maybe playing a team like Texas when they sit in a zone. If you get by the first round you could get beat by a very good team in the second game. But if you're the No. 1 pick and you lose in the first or second round, it almost would be a disaster. Every time the media asked me about it, I'd never say that to them. I'd talk about the season and the journey. But deep down, you are worried about it."

The three Illini assistant coaches - Wayne McClain, Jay Price and Tracy Webster - rotate preparing the scouting reports on Illinois' opponents. If a coach has had success with a team in the past, he'll retain that team as his "scout" the next time around. And those scouting reports become the basis for Illinois' strategy. McClain said Weber gives his assistant coaches great latitude in preparing the reports.

"He trusts us completely. Thoroughly. One hundred percent," McClain said. "It's a good feeling. If he wants to tweak something, we understand that. He's the head coach. You bring him a plan, you suggest things and you can't have an ego in this thing. And I don't think he does, either. Sometimes we say, 'Let's do it like this,' and he'll say no. But the good thing is, during a game you can turn to him and say, 'Coach, I really think we need to do it like this,' and he'll say, 'OK, make your adjustments.' He's real good. I've never had a guy like that."

Throughout this unique season, there was mounting pressure on the assistants not to be the one whose scouting report resulted in the team's first loss. "Oh, man, that was pressure," McClain said. "It's a strange feeling. That's the competitiveness of everyone. It's not like you want anyone to lose, but you sure don't want it to be your scout. But that's not fair because you might land some of the tougher teams. Did we lose at Ohio State because of the scouting report? Absolutely not. We led the game by 11 in the second half. We just didn't execute down the stretch. You try to do the scouting reports on teams you're comfortable with or might have a little inside track on. I didn't have Gonzaga or Wake Forest, but I had Arkansas and Cincinnati. I had Cincinnati because I had them in the NCAA Tournament the year before. If we had played Kansas, I guarantee you I would have had Kansas because I'd been on Bill Self's staff. You like to think you can get inside their minds a little bit."

When Illinois' first NCAA Tournament game finally arrived, many of Weber's fears were realized. "You could see one of the effects of that No. 1 vs. No. 16 stuff. They came out and played loose and free. We played tight and now you start thinking and worrying. Finally we just kind of turned it out. Then it was just getting through the game and moving on."

Illinois struggled through a poor first-half performance and led by just a single point at halftime. A 14-2 run early in the second half was the difference in a 67-55 victory, led by Dee Brown's 19 points. James Augustine added 11 points and 15 rebounds. But Weber's thoughts about an Illini-Texas showdown in the second game never materialized when Nevada dumped the Longhorns 61-57.

Weber repeatedly said he worried about his team when it played against opponents it didn't know or didn't respect. But his players, who he called "basketball worldly," held a genuine respect for

Nevada because they remembered what the Wolfpack had accomplished the season before. Nevada had defeated Kansas in the regular season, then knocked off both Michigan State and Gonzaga to advance as a No. 10 seed to the Sweet 16 of the NCAA Tournament. "Our players probably knew more about them than we did," Weber said. "Normally you might have to search for it and find it, that something that could get them motivated to play at a high level. But we didn't have to go overboard to motivate them for this one."

The report on Nevada emphasized the skill of their big forwards, Nick Fazekas and Kevinn Pinckney. But assistant coach Jay Price felt Illinois could attack their strength, and James Augustine, playing what Weber called "probably his best game of the season," teamed with Jack Ingram to give Nevada fits.

Augustine had 23 points, 10 rebounds and four steals, while Ingram came off the bench to hit six of seven shots for 12 points as Illinois won 71-59. "We challenged James and he really rose to the occasion offensive and defensively. We thought we could score on them inside, and James just got on a roll. And he guarded the heck out of Fazekas. He just frustrated him. James was the most dominant player in the game."

Illinois also got an assist from the crowd. "Thursday was good, but Saturday, with Kentucky and Cincinnati playing in the other game, the crowd was unbelievable (40,311). It set a record and it was amazing because there was orange everywhere. It was like revisiting the Big Ten Tournament. There were people everywhere. A lot of people had gambled and bought tickets ahead of time, hoping we'd be there. It was almost like playing in Assembly Hall."

All along, Weber had hoped for the Indianapolis assignment because the Regional games were in Chicago and the Final Four, of course, was in St. Louis. He called the prospect of traveling so close to Champaign "the bus route," and now it was time to head to the Allstate Arena in Rosemont, the western Chicago suburb. The arena was much smaller than a dome, but the atmosphere would be out of this world. Little did anyone know the excitement that awaited the 34-1 Illini in the Windy City.

CHAPTER TWENTY

ON TO CHICAGO

Fans argue for hours about which teams will advance in the NCAA

Tournament, and they'll stare holes in their bracket sheets trying to

foresee upsets and predict which teams will advance all the way to

the Final Four. They will anticipate match-ups and ask, 'what if"

every step of the way, cross-checking teams and looking for obstacles

and pitfalls. Coaches would like you to believe they don't look ahead

when it comes to their Tournament fate, but that's probably not

quite true. Most coaches can't resist the temptation to peek and

wonder and see exactly who could be lurking down the road. But in

Bruce Weber's case, he swears he made a pledge he was able to keep.

"After we beat Nevada we were pretty fired up, thinking about

going to Chicago. I kind of knew who was in our bracket, but I did-

n't know exactly who was there. I really didn't. I'd told the kids to

go one step at a time, and I tried to practice what I preached to the

kids." Weber's theory: If you don't come ready to play today, you

won't get to play tomorrow.

"So after the Nevada game, Kent Brown grabbed me and took me to the TV interview and said, 'Guess who you could be playing.' The game between Boston College and Wisconsin-Milwaukee was still going on, but by the time the interview had ended, Wisconsin-Milwaukee had won it. That was my alma mater, but it was also the school where Bruce Pearl was coaching, and Kent said, 'Oh, my God, our fans will be going crazy.'"

Pearl was an assistant coach at the University of Iowa when he became a central figure in what can politely be called "the Deon Thomas investigation." That incident permanently stamped Pearl as a man Illini fans love to hate, a label even he would acknowledge in the days leading up to the Regional opener.

Weber knew questions about Pearl would be coming, so he pulled his team together and gave them a brief description of what happened, telling them to answer the questions truthfully - that they really didn't know anything about it, the matter took place when they were too young to understand and their real focus needed to be on a Wisconsin-Milwaukee team that had just knocked off Alabama and Boston College. Weber knew one thing for certain: Spend too

BRUCE WEBER WITH MARK TUPPER

much time worrying about what happened in 1990 and fail to adequately prepare for a red-hot 2005 Wisconsin-Milwaukee team, and fans would never forgive him.

"I down-played it to the media, but deep down I would joke with the staff and say, 'It's the 100th anniversary of Illinois basketball and it's going to go down as a tremendous season, and I'm going to lose to Bruce Pearl, the coach Illinois fans hate more than any other.' We joked about it, but it really wasn't funny. Wisconsin-Milwaukee is hard to play."

Unbeknownst to the public, there was another factor that made Weber uneasy. During practice in Champaign early in the week, Luther Head strained his hamstring and for the first time all season a starter's effectiveness was in doubt.

"We'd been lucky all year with injuries," Weber said. "Other than Brian Randle, the only thing we really had was in Iowa when Rich McBride missed the game with an illness. But here we are in the Regionals and we really need Luther against UW-M."

It was time for trainer Al Martindale to work his magic. "They started doing a bunch of treatments and we kept him out of practice," Weber said. "Then I found out he'd had the same problem early in the season. That was refreshing. I didn't even know he'd had it, but he fought through it. The thing with hamstrings is you just never know. And when we went to the shootaround at Allstate the day before the game, they had the hockey ice under the court and the building was just freezing. He could hardly do anything in the shootaround. I was worried, but Luther kept saying, 'Coach, I'll be OK. I played the whole year (as a sophomore) with tears in my abdomen, and I can play with this.' But still, you just don't know."

Weber was familiar with Wisconsin-Milwaukee's style of play, and he could understand why Alabama and Boston College had been caught by surprise. "They play a very chaotic style, something you're not used to seeing in college basketball. They try to make you play faster than you want. I played them when I was at Southern. And Bruce Pearl had come from the Tom Davis system, and of course I played against that when Bruce was an assistant at Iowa and I was an assistant at Purdue. So I was familiar with their stuff."

It turned out to be an intense game, and the emotional undercurrent of Pearl's presence was only one factor for the fans. Weber and the players had their hands full on the court. "It was a very hard-fought game. They kept coming at us and never let us rest. That's what we expected. Our kids - I don't know if it was the adrenalin of it and the arena and the crowd - but when we were done we were just exhausted. Fighting against their press, we'd make runs but they never quit. Whenever we made a run they answered. Finally, we kind of broke them.

"Luther was fine for about three-quarters of the game. Then he went in for a lay-up and got twisted a little, and you could see the rest of the game it was hard for him. He had to fight through it. But I do remember he pulled up and made a huge jump shot."

The result was a 77-63 Illini victory sparked by Deron Williams and Dee Brown, who combined for 42 points to send Illinois winging into the Elite Eight. That accomplished the goal of advancing further than the team had the previous season, but by hanging the Final Four logo in the locker room before the year began, Weber already had sent the message that the Elite Eight was not enough.

This was St. Louis or bust.

During stoppages in the Wisconsin-Milwaukee game, the attention turned to the stands directly behind the Illini bench. That's where actor/comedian Bill Murray was whooping it up with Illini fans. Murray, an Illinois native, had clearly become caught up in the excitement of the tournament, and his presence seemed to add a layer of celebrity to a team that already was commanding the spotlight on its own.

"When I got back to the hotel that night someone comes up and says, 'Bill Murray wants to meet you,'" Weber said. "He was in the lobby bar and the hotel lobby was pretty crowded. I asked if he would mind coming up here and he said he would. When this happens, my wife starts telling me that he was with her and the kids and was just unbelievable with the crowd during the game. Here is this famous person and he wants to come talk to me? I'm intimidated by him more than anything. But he was hilarious. He was great with the kids. He wanted to know about our team and the fans. He talked about his enjoyment of the game. We sat there for a half hour or 40 minutes.

"At the end he started talking about the pictures he took with my daughters. He made them do cross-eyed pictures, just a fun thing." Murray had told Weber's youngest daughter, Emily, that she had "the best cross eyes in the world," which only encouraged her posing. Normally that would be fine. But Megan Weber cringed because Emily had undergone eye surgery as a youngster and was supposed to avoid unnecessary eye strain.

"I asked him, 'What was your most famous movie?' He said it was *All About Bob*. Then he started talking about the season and how it's long and hard and it's the same way when you make a movie. He talked about filming that movie, and every day after filming was done, some local guy would bring them moonshine. We joked that Gary Nottingham was from West Virginia and he knew people who made moonshine. And he said he'd like to meet him. So Gary's wife, Paulina, who was there, runs and gets Gary, and Gary tells stories about moonshine. It was crazy.

"Then he asked, 'Is there anything I could do for you?' I asked if he would like to talk to our team, and I told him he could do it after practice the next day. He didn't commit, but the next day, all of a sudden he shows up at Allstate Arena and no one can get him in because he doesn't have a credential. Hey, it's Bill Murray! I think Ron Guenther finally got him in after he said he was coming to see our team. The NCAA told him if he talked to our team he had to talk to Arizona, too. Can you believe that? By the time he finally got into the arena, the team had gone back to the hotel. I had to stay around with Kent and do some things and while we're driving back, who do we see? It's Bill Murray, walking along the street back to the hotel. He'd gone to the Target store by the arena and bought this rubber ball, and he was just walking along, bouncing the ball. I didn't know why but I found out later."

Just when the team was preparing to leave the hotel for dinner, Bill Murray strolled in ready to address the team. For the time being, dinner would wait.

"What happened next was unbelievable. The ball was a prop. Right away he starts flinging it at people, just a fun thing to see if someone was paying attention. It was funny. He talked about making a movie, how hard it gets, how you have to stick together and fight through to the finish. It was a good message. He's such an amazing people person. Just from watching our guys in games, he knew their individual personalities. Right away he went after Nick, massaging him, trying to get him to smile, sitting on his lap. I guess he had done a role as a Chinese masseuse so he took on that character. Nick stood up, and Bill said, 'Oh, is that all you?'

"He let the kids ask questions, and Dee asked about *Caddy Shack* and he did Carl Spackler," the character he made famous in the classic comedy. "My wife walked in a little late and she's trying to sneak in but he sees her and flings the ball at her. And she doesn't catch it, so he says, 'Coach Weber's wife doesn't have good hands.' It was supposed to be 10 minutes, but it was at least a half-hour. And it was good. That's something we won't forget, and it came at a good time because it just loosened everyone up."

Murray thought the Wisconsin-Milwaukee game was tremendous. But what he witnessed the next day was off the charts.

CHAPTER TWENTY-ONE

THE COMEBACK

Atop Bruce Weber's desk at the Ubben Basketball Complex sits a small rock paperweight with an inspirational inscription that speaks to him every day: "Winners never quit. Quitters never win." For a man who competes every day of his life, and who does so with a burning urgency only his closest friends understand, those words define him.

Late Thursday evening, after Illinois had disposed of Wisconsin-Milwaukee, the Allstate Arena crowd was busy watching one whale of a nightcap as Arizona and Oklahoma State - two college basketball heavyweights - tangled for an Elite Eight berth and the right to face Illinois on Saturday.

It was a fiercely competitive game, one that felt destined to come down to a final shot. It did, of course, with Arizona's dead-eye shooter Salim Stoudamire nailing a cold-blooded, off-balance jumper with 2.8 seconds left to lift Arizona to a 79-78 victory over the Cowboys.

And so there it was again, Illinois vs. Arizona for the right to advance to the Final Four, just as it had been March 25, 2001, in San Antonio, the day Arizona held on in a brutally physical game to win 87-81. There had been tears and long faces that day, and Illini fans remembered all too well the disappointment of pulling up short with so much at stake. Could Bruce Weber and this Illini team make them forget about that pain? Weber knew very early it would be a most difficult task.

"The thing was, you knew Oklahoma State was good," Weber said. "Those guys had played a great game. Then you start studying the stats and you realize Stoudamire shoots 50 percent from 3 and (Channing) Frye and the others are so athletic."

When preparing for a game, the Illini coaching staff pays special attention to an opponent's last four games. They want to know how a team is playing lately, what they're doing now, who's been hot over the past two weeks, who's in a recent slump, and what tendencies a coach is leaning on at this point in the season. "We also like to find teams who have beaten them or played very well against them. When we prepared for Cincinnati, we watched UAB (Alabama-Birmingham) because they had beaten them. UAB's quickness hurt Cincinnati. They got them running. So for Arizona, we watched Washington State because Coach Bennett beat them once, and their other game went to overtime. But even watching that we were thinking, 'God, these guys are good.' And Frye played unbelievable the whole weekend. I had NBA guys tell me they'd seen him for five years and could not imagine him playing at that high a level."

In the time between the Wisconsin-Milwaukee game and the showdown with Arizona, trainer Al Martindale's chief responsibility was to do everything in his power to make sure Luther Head's sore hamstring could withstand another physical test. Martindale administered a battery of treatments - massages, stretching, work in the hotel swimming pool - all designed to ensure that Head could answer the bell. More important, he wanted to make sure Head could still be on the court when the final buzzer sounded. Publicly, Weber said he was prepared to do without Head if the hamstring injury flared up. Privately, he doubted Illinois could win without him.

The Allstate Arena was packed, and just as Weber hoped, orange ruled the day. Illini fans were everywhere, cascading from the rafters like a spilled orange slushy. And just as he'd been for the Wisconsin-Milwaukee game, Bill Murray was situated behind the Illini bench, his head bobbing up and down in nervous anticipation. During their face-to-face meeting, Murray had described himself to Weber as a "casual" Illini fan, a guy who rooted quietly from afar because he'd been born in Illinois and felt some affection for the state school. Clearly, though, Murray had been transformed, and if Weber had needed an extra body to bump chests with Channing Frye, Murray would have been among the first to volunteer.

Those not lucky enough to have a ticket were gathered around televisions, radios and Internet feeds around the world. We know this now because before this historic Saturday was through, fans would be reaching out to share with the world their experiences on a day they said they would never forget.

"I thought we played pretty good," Weber said of Illinois' performance in the early stretches of the game. "It was a typical game. We had good feelings about it going in and we kept getting little runs. Right before halftime we made a nice run, then we screwed up and they scored a bucket just before half." Still, Illinois led 38-36, and Head's tender hamstring was still intact.

"But they scored the first basket of the second half and then it was like we just couldn't stop them," Weber said. "We kept scoring, too, and for the first 10 minutes of the second half it was back and forth, back and forth. But it always seemed - you know, mentally, in my mind as a coach - that they were in control. We're in Allstate Arena, we have the fans and yet they're controlling the tempo of the game. It seemed like when we got to the 10-minute mark we rushed some shots, we weren't as patient, and they had every answer. They hit everything. They did everything right. It happened from like nine minutes to about 4:30, and their big spurt was the last six or seven points. It happened very quickly."

Sure enough, with 9:22 remaining in the second half, Arizona's lead was a mere three points, 60-57. But over the next six minutes, the Wildcats would pull out to a 75-60 lead, a 15-point margin that pinned stunned fans back into their seats, and left Illinois with a monumental mountain to climb. "Arizona has exploded to a 15-point lead!" exclaimed CBS's Dick Enberg as he called the game from courtside.

Down 15 points. Four minutes to go. A season so filled with wonderful moments and so many precise plays teetered on the brink of collapse. Weber said a thousands things flooded through his mind during those seconds, one of which was, "How the heck am I going to get out of here alive?" He knew how much this game meant to his players, to his staff and to that throng of fans who had been so wonderfully supportive all season. It couldn't end now, not here, not in this sea of orange waiting for the slightest sign to bring them to their feet again. This dream season couldn't slip away now, before leading the Illini to the glistening St. Louis Arch, could it?

A 3-pointer by Deron Williams cut the lead to 75-63, but seconds later James Augustine picked up a foul, his fifth, and shuffled to the bench. Less than three-and-a-half minutes to go. A pair of free throws by McClellan made it 77-63, and Head answered with a 3-pointer to close it to 77-66. With 2:43 to play, Head missed a 3-pointer, but Jack Ingram, whose role in the game became huge with

Augustine on the bench, tapped the rebound against the backboard and Dee Brown grabbed it, scoring on a little floater in the lane that cut Arizona's lead to 77-68. And during the ensuing timeout, Weber realized his team needed to be reminded about the rock that sits atop his desk.

"During a timeout you say so many things," he recalled. "They all had their heads down. I said, 'Look at me, guys. Look in my eyes. What we've done is unbelievable, but don't go down and be a quitter. Let's battle! Let's fight!'"

It was also during a late timeout that Illinois made a strategic defensive adjustment, something assistant coach Wayne McClain said they'd worked on for weeks and saved for a rainy day. Well, it was pouring.

"I remember us telling Bruce, 'Hey, coach, we have to start pressing,'" McClain recalled. "Because we hadn't done it all year. It's something we talked about all the time but never used it. When are we going to use it? We're down. We called the press 'twenty-two' because it was a 2-2-1, and one of the kids suggested, 'Let's just call it 22.' That was easy to remember. We put it in during a time when we had a full week off. Boy, talk about a savior. That was it."

When Illinois walked onto the floor following the timeout, McClain saw one of the many "little" things Ingram did in those final moments. "A lot of people don't even realize it, but Jack goes back out there and puts his arms up to get the crowd back into it. The crowd had gotten quiet. And they responded to that and guys just started making plays."

Make plays they did, magically, in rapid-fire succession. With the press suddenly clogging passing lanes, Illinois started to get deflections and steals. And from the bench Weber said he could feel the noise level rise and the momentum start to shift. A deflection by Ingram resulted in Head's steal and lay-up that made it 77-70. But only 1:18 remained, and Weber could feel each tick of the clock. Arizona's Jawaan McClellan hit a free throw to make it 78-70, but Deron Williams found the strength to fly the length of the court, laying it in to make it 78-72.

By now the Allstate Arena crowd had gone to the whip and the roar in the darkened building was building louder by the second. With 1:03 to go, Brown intentionally fouled Mustafa Shakur, and he swished both free throws to put Arizona on top 80-72. Then, with 54 seconds to play, Head, playing valiantly on a hamstring that was burning, drilled a 3-pointer from the left wing, making it 80-75. By now the "22" press had unnerved Arizona, and Brown slapped the ball away from Shakur. Williams gathered it in and fed it ahead to Brown, who dropped it in to make it a one-possession game, 80-77. The Allstate Arena is directly adjacent to O'Hare International Airport and at times, the jets seem to scrape across the roof on their flight paths. Now, however, the noise inside the building is louder than anything that could be happening in the flyway. CBS' Jay Bilas remarks, "Illinois is showing the heart of a champion!"

With 45 seconds to go, Arizona coach Lute Olson calls timeout, and when Illinois returns to the floor, Weber walks several feet onto the playing surface to survey the Wildcats' personnel. "Sometimes I'll do that. I'll go way out on the court and make the refs push me off, and when I got out there I moved Jack up to watch Frye and he ended up making the steal." Ingram's key deflection of the inbounds pass went to Head, who passed up a 3-pointer in order to get Illinois into its offense. Looking back, the comeback was not only about shots made. It was in part about shots passed up, which was fitting since throughout the season the effectiveness of the Illinois offense was based on this very unselfishness.

The ball ended up going to Williams, who had been doing such a stifling defensive job on Stoudamire, and rather than instinctively launch the first 3-point look he had, Williams instead cut behind a hard screen by Ingram and snapped off a 3-pointer that drained through the net, tying the game 80-80 and sending the crowd into an uncontrolled frenzy.

"One of the Arizona assistant coaches told me two weeks later when we were out recruiting that when Deron hit that shot, he swears he felt the building move," Weber said. "It was absolutely rocking. It was so loud in there. I think our kids just felt we were going to win the game. That was an incredible moment."

Incredible, yes, but Illinois erased Arizona's 15-point lead almost too quickly. There were still 39 seconds to play and despite a sub-par shooting game, Stoudamire was still one of the game's best with the outcome hanging in the balance. Weber remembered all too well what he'd done to Oklahoma State just two days earlier.

"Our last eight points came so fast," Weber said. "The last thing we did at our shootaround was talk about how they go to Stoudamire at the end. We talked about it a lot as a staff, and we said we would run someone at Stoudamire and not let him beat us. But they never really went to him."

Instead, McClellan missed a jumper from the left baseline, and Dee Brown grabbed the rebound with several seconds remaining. "Dee turned and saw Deron, who was wide open at the other end. If Dee can throw the ball to him, Deron has a dead lay-up. It's amazing. And Luther is running at the ref trying to call timeout. But Dee throws it, and the ball gets deflected and goes to Stoudamire. Oh, no! Stoudamire is going to get the shot anyway. But Luther does something that reminded me of that game last year at Purdue, when we clinched the Big Ten championship. Remember? Luther runs all the way from half-court and gets the putback basket. Well, this time he's trying to call timeout and sees the ball get deflected and everyone else is standing around stunned. But Luther, he flies in

BRUCE WEBER WITH MARK TUPPER

174

there and blocks Stoudamire's shot. Even with the bad hamstring, Luther is the guy still making plays."

Head's block forced overtime and both teams were gasping for breath. If there ever was a moment when Weber's run-run-run conditioning program pays off, it is this moment. "From here on it was like a heavyweight boxing match with both teams hanging on the ropes, trying to fight through to the end," Weber said. "And again, it all came down to the end."

Head, the tireless one playing on guts, heart and a leg that feels like it's been stabbed with a kitchen knife, steals the ball and scores on a breakaway to put Illinois on top 90-84 with 1:57 left in overtime. Every player on the floor is physically better off than Head, but the guy who always led Weber's distance runs is the one with gas in his tank. Two inside baskets and a free throw by Hassan Adams, who played so brilliantly in this game, sliced Illinois' lead to one point, 90-89. And when Arizona called timeout with 11 seconds to go, Weber once again figured he'd have to deal with Stoudamire's jump shot.

But as he scanned his valiant team, he saw pain and incredible fatigue. "I'm in the huddle asking guys who can make a play. Luther has the bad leg. Guys are cramping. We found out later Deron had injured his foot. Dee was cramping. James had fouled out. Roger can't really create. And Deron was hurting so bad he said he didn't think he could take Stoudamire. He was hurting the most. I'm not kidding, at this point both teams were just hanging on each other.

"I knew Deron was hurting, but he's also our smartest player. So we switched Luther onto Stoudamire and told Deron he was the guy who'd have to run at him. We just didn't want him to be the guy to beat us. But I guess in their minds, Stoudamire was 2-for-13 shooting, so…. We put Deron on Adams and the ball goes to Adams and that's a great matchup for Deron. He's quicker. When the ball went to Adams I'm thinking, 'OK, high-low' because Frye was down there. But he came out and I thought, 'Oh, they're clearing out.' But Adams held onto the ball. And you're watching the play and you're watching the clock and all of a sudden I'm thinking, 'He might not even get the shot off!' And then he has to throw a 3 up there and it misses and I realize we won."

Gary Nottingham, whose official title is assistant to the head coach, was the first to throw his arms around Weber. If you ever see a photo of that moment, there is an explosion of emotions and tears between two men who have known each other since they were graduate assistants at Western Kentucky. "Gary is probably the most unemotional guy on our staff, him and Wayne, and that kind of showed you," Weber said. "For him, what he's come through, a long time in Division II, now to be going to the Final Four and to be a part of it, he was just in tears and he wouldn't let go. At first I didn't even know who was grabbing me. Then I tried to make sure I got to each coach. And then you try to get your sense about yourself.

"After we shook Arizona's hands, now your guys are running all over the place. It was just crazy. I know I hugged a bunch of people. My first thought was about my wife and kids. But they'd already been escorted down. I found them and hugged them. Somehow my older brother, Ron, got down there and we hugged and that was pretty emotional because of my mom and everything. There's a picture of us that has been in a lot of magazines and newspapers. Every magazine says it was Dave, but it wasn't. It was Ron."

It seemed like everyone was dancing and jumping and hugging and crying. But over on the Illinois bench, one man remained seated. "It was surreal," assistant coach Wayne McClain said. "I just sat there and didn't move. It was hard to believe you could do that. It was against all odds. Against a good team in the double bonus with great guards, a team that was handling us. They were taking us to the woodshed for a while there. I just sat there and took it all in. I couldn't believe what just happened. I still can't."

About the time Illinois fell behind by 15 points, McClain saw two things he felt might give Illinois a chance. "I saw Arizona celebrating just a little bit out on the court. They were feeling it and smiling. One of the Arizona players said, 'Four more minutes to St. Louis.' And they brought out boxes with the Regional championship T-shirts and caps and placed them behind the Arizona bench. Then with about one minute to go, after we'd cut their lead down, they came back and grabbed the boxes and took them away. I think they figured out maybe the game wasn't over after all."

The game has subsequently been described as one of the greatest NCAA Tournament games in history, perhaps one of the great college basketball comebacks of all time. Most athletic department insiders now view it as the greatest game in the 100-year history of Illinois basketball.

"I've been in a couple of crazy games, but for that magnitude, with so much on the line, and that comeback in such a short period of time...," Weber said. "It just tells you never to give up, never to quit. I don't think there's any doubt that when they do something about special moments in the NCAA Tournament that thing will go down as one of the most special games of all time. There wasn't the one signature play, but the game itself was one of the best.

"There were a lot of people tied to us nationally. People kind of jumped on our bandwagon. I think in a way we became America's team. I'm not saying that in a cocky way, but we were the team that didn't get a lot of respect, the team everyone was waiting for to falter, we played the way people like a team to play and it all played into the emotion of that game."

Back on the University of Illinois campus, happy students and fans were literally dancing in the streets. It was a celebration that would go on deep into the next morning. Meanwhile, an exhilarated and exhausted Illini team finally boarded the bus for the drive back to Champaign. Weber, however, had to stay behind to accommodate extra media requests. So he and his wife, Megan, waited and drove back alone.

"Kent Brown was the first one who called and he said, 'You have to catch up with the team bus.' Then Al Martindale called and said, 'People are already out on the highway and they're lining up at Ubben.' I hadn't eaten all day. I got some snacks in the car and they called again from the team bus and said they were getting a police escort. I said, 'Can someone get one for me?' I just started going 80, 85 miles an hour trying to catch them."

The Webers still trailed the team bus when they sped down I-57 and passed Highway 9 at Paxton, where fans and emergency vehicles lined the overpass to celebrate Illinois' first trip to the Final Four since 1989. He finally caught the bus at University Avenue and when they pulled closer to the Ubben Basketball Complex, the sight gave them chills.

"It was just amazing at Ubben," Weber said. "There were thousands of people. I stayed until 2:30 in the morning and those people would have stayed all night. I had been on the phone the whole way home and when I got out of our car they gave me a microphone and I literally couldn't talk. My lips moved but nothing came out. It was cold and wet and people were going nuts."

Eventually, the Webers headed home, only to spot people running around on their lawn. Momentarily frightened, they phoned the police. "Dana Brenner (one of Ron Guenther's top assistants) had told us one time if something like that ever happens to call the police and have them come out. So we called the police and it turns out it was Dana's daughters and a bunch of my older daughter's friends. They were running around putting signs up on the house, welcoming and congratulating us. Now the police are coming and it's these kids we know. We felt bad afterward."

As physically and mentally drained as he was, Bruce Weber did not sleep the night of the miracle comeback against Arizona. "It was already four in the morning. I made a pizza and was watching SportsCenter, wanting to see the highlights. I started doing the laundry. I had to be on early in the morning with ESPN or some-thing, and I don't ever remember laying down. I did go to church, though.

"Toward the end of the season Dr. Kyrouac had given me some sleeping pills, and I had one extra one. Megan couldn't sleep, so I cut the last one in half and gave it to her. So in the morning I get up and do the ESPN thing and another radio interview and I go to church. She was going to meet me. It's Easter Sunday, and I'm waiting and waiting and she slept right through it.

"So I go get the dogs from the people who take care of them and now it's noon, so I call the house. I said, 'Do you need anything from the store.' Megan said, 'We'll go after church.' I said, 'Would you look at the clock? It's already noon.'"

"I went to the grocery story and I still remember this. I was trying to get a few things so we'd have some food for Easter and everyone starts clapping. All of a sudden everyone stopped and started clap-ping. All these people came from all over the store. I got a standing ovation at the supermarket. It was really neat. To get that response at the store, that was really something."

Really something? To have played a game that will be talked about generations from now, and to have it stamp Illinois' ticket to the Final Four, yes, that was really something. It was a game that will forever define a team that was, to say the least, really something.

CHAPTER TWENTY-TWO

FINALLY, THE FINAL FOUR

Bruce Weber does some of his best thinking when he walks, at times alone late, late at night, scooting along with the dogs, working his cell phone and leaving messages for people who long ago have hit their pillows. He and Megan like to walk together in the morning, knowing it's often the only time they can share in the heart of the season.

"On the day of the Arizona game, I was walking thinking about a lot of things," Weber said. "I don't know when Coach Keady called, but he called over that weekend and I'd been thinking, 'Man, if I get to go to the Final Four and he never got to go, I don't know if that's fair.' I heard (Michigan State's) Tom Izzo talk about it, but at least Jud Heathcote got to go. I called Coach, and he told me his wife was crying watching the Arizona game. He was so happy for us. And then he kind of grumbled, joking with me, 'Yeah, and now I have to introduce you for a bunch of your dang awards.' Sure enough, he was the guy who introduced me at two of the national

BRUCE WEBER WITH MARK TUPPER

Coach of the Year things. It was pretty neat to have him do that."

Weber had worried for some time about the overwhelming hoopla associated with a trip to the Final Four. He had called coaches like Izzo, Connecticut's Jim Calhoun, Utah's Rick Majerus and one of the Marquette assistants to find out what routines worked and what didn't during their Final Four visits. His own experience was complicated because he would receive eight national Coach of the Year awards in all, many of which included ceremonies in St. Louis. Weber, of course, was expected to attend every one.

Add to that the absolutely frantic fan following that now waited in hotel lobbies, outside arena entrances and near the team bus to get a handshake, a photo or perhaps a treasured autograph. The Illini team had dealt with this all season, and it had become common for autograph hounds to be waiting by players' cars when practice was finished. They didn't mind signing for kids and loyal fans who truly valued each memento, but too many of the items were being sold on the Internet, and they soon began to recognize the faces of those hired by sales agents to secure signatures for profit.

Weber is a natural sucker for autograph seekers. He has a habit of signing not only his name, but greetings like "Go Illini!" and "Final 4, '05," and often he'll do it in both blue and orange markers, personalizing the message with the person's name. "If you're really giving someone an autograph, you want it to be something special," he said of his signature signing philosophy. "Not just a scribble. I just know that when I was a kid, when I got an autograph I at least wanted to be able to read it. The players make fun of me constantly, but the crazy thing is, they all started doing some of the stuff I did. I realize there's a point when you can't do it, but I feel bad when I can't do something.

"I think through the tournament our kids were great. They signed an astronomical number of autographs. They were all so cordial, such good guys, but you get stuck trying to practice or watch film or go to dinner. That's where Rod (Cardinal) and Dana (Brenner) did such an unbelievable job. Even before we beat Fairleigh Dickinson they made plans for the whole thing. They set up security and visited hotels in St. Louis. They had buses waiting underground, had us sneaking out of back doors and everything. They really did a great job planning it all out."

The city of St. Louis greeted the Final Four with warm and open arms, and among Weber's greatest memories of the entire season was the nighttime view of the Arch as the team bus crossed the glistening Mississippi River. "Deron Williams likes to make fun of me all the time, and I remember Deron yelling on the bus, 'Coach, could you move? Your head is blocking the dome.'"

It was Weber's decision to let the team stay downtown, and the Marriott across the street from Busch Stadium became the Illini headquarters. "I didn't realize how many Illinois fans would be coming and how crazy it would be. Coach Calhoun said to let the players enjoy it. Part of the thing is the tickets. That's a major deal. I told them, set a goal. By noon on Tuesday, be done with your tickets." Each player gets six tickets, so distributing a limited number shouldn't be that difficult. For Weber, however, it was a greater chore.

Because he felt he owed so many family and friends a chance to see this historic moment, Weber sought out tickets wherever he could find them. "I bought tickets from the Missouri Valley Conference people, they helped me. And I kept buying them from people when they lost. I probably had 60-some. I wanted some for SIU players who wanted to go. I got our old trainer at SIU and his wife tickets. Kevin Stallings helped me get some, too."

With all the commotion regarding tickets, coaching awards, the pomp and circumstance of merely arriving and the growing crush of fans, preparing for the games may have seemed secondary. Again, that's where Weber's staff was working overtime, perfecting their scouting reports and making sure loose ends were securely fastened.

On the same day Illinois had rallied from 15 down to upend Arizona, Louisville had raced from 20 points behind to squeeze past West Virginia 93-85 in overtime. Louisville was streaming along, hot as blazes, having won 13 in a row, including impressive NCAA tournament wins against Georgia Tech and Washington prior to the West Virginia thriller. And, of course, there was the aura of the Louisville coach, Rick Pitino, who was making his fifth Final Four appearance, who had won the national title while coaching Kentucky in 1996 and who had been head coach of both the Boston Celtics and New York Knicks.

"The only times I coached against him was when I was an assistant at Purdue and we played them when he was head coach at Boston U. We played them at their place, and we beat them. And we played them when he had his real good Kentucky team, with Antoine Walker, and we didn't beat them."

On Friday, the day before the semifinal game against Louisville, each team practiced in the Edward Jones Dome, a mostly-for-show event that is open to the public. It's a chance to get a feel for the shooting background, but mostly it's a chance to strut and preen in front of a crowd. The crowd that awaited the Illini was large and loud.

"I told them, 'You have to understand there's going to be 20,000 people there. For a practice you're going to be amazed.' Our guys started peeking out and came running back into our locker room. 'It's almost full! It's almost full!' We had no idea." To Weber, this helped justify the conversations he'd shared with coaches who had Final Four experience. "One of the things they all said was, 'Your kids are going to hit a point of being overwhelmed and you have to hope it comes before the game. I think it was one of the Marquette assistants who said that moment for them came during the Kansas game (when Marquette was blown out). The guys I talked to said you have to talk about it, talk about it so it becomes something in their head. So I talked to our team about it so they'd know what to expect."

In preparing for the game, Weber and his staff went through their usual routine, which included looking closely at the last four games and examining film of a team that beat or gave Louisville trouble. It was a tape of Memphis beating Louisville earlier in the season that gave the Illini staff some clues about how to attack Pitino's defense. And the decision was made to give Deron Williams the defensive assignment against Louisville's explosive Francisco Garcia.

"The thing with Deron was, as a freshman and sophomore, he was our best defensive player," Weber said. "As a junior, all of a sudden he was an offensive player, and mentally he lost his pride in his defensive work. He got mad at us for telling him that, but it was true. He was having trouble earlier in the year, so we switched Luther onto their best players. But now, Luther's injury was a factor. It started with (Ed) McCants of Wisconsin-Milwaukee and then

Stoudamire and now it really meant something for Deron, too. He had his ego jilted a little. We wouldn't let him guard the best players. We all thought that would be a good matchup, Deron on Garcia. Deron was strong, he had pretty good size and he could get into him. Deron just never let him get involved. Garcia didn't even take bad shots. Deron just stymied him, the same as he did with Stoudamire."

Garcia had scored 23 points against Washington, 21 against Georgia Tech and opened the NCAA tournament with 27 against Louisiana-Lafayette. Against Illinois, Garcia scored four, making just two of his 10 shots.

"They were good, but those others guys played off him and their big guys were role players, just like our big guys," Weber said. "Guarding him was a big key, that and dealing with their zone. When we had the bye at the end of the season, we sat down as a staff and talked about what we needed to do. The consensus was, we could play Syracuse or someone like that in the tournament and see a zone. I had some stuff I'd gotten from (Army Coach) Jim Crews, something from the Purdue days, and we put in some new zone stuff, probably six weeks before the Louisville game. We practiced that the whole time but never used it.

"So when we got to Louisville we ran some stuff they couldn't have seen on film. And it helped us. It gave us some easy looks and gave them some things to think about. I think it gave our kids a chance. It was still close until Roger had that crazy start to the second half. He had that follow dunk that made all the highlight reels. When you talk about someone playing at that special level, on that night it was him. Roger got us going, and I thought they froze. And once they had to go to man-to-man, it was over. Our kids were like, 'This is easy.' It was almost like our defense got better as the game went on. They only scored, what, 57 points? You think about that. That's pretty good against a team that scores a ton of points." Indeed, a Louisville team that had scored 93 points in each of its two previous games sputtered offensively as Illinois won 72-57.

As well as Illinois played defensively, the game was not decided until the second half, when Powell scored nine straight points to help Illinois take control. Not until a breakaway burst after holding a 50-

49 lead did Weber began to breathe a sigh of relief. Powell sandwiched a layup and a jumper around a pair of 3-pointers by Luther Head as part of an 11-0 run. The play fans were howling about came when Powell missed an open 3, then charged the basket and emphatically dunked home the rebound as Illinois won for the 37th time, tying the NCAA record for most victories in a season. Powell and Head each finished with 20 points, and Williams had nine assists and five rebounds to go with his lock-down defensive gem against Garcia.

"I think the neatest moment was the last 15 seconds of the Louisville game," Weber said. "You kind of had time to sit there, dribbling it out, to look around and feel it and know you're going to be playing in the national championship game. And to watch the highlight tape and to hear (CBS') Jim Nantz saying, 'They've been going since October 15th and now, for the first time in school history, in the championship game!" The crowd was going nuts, and you could suck it all in. You could feel it. After the game, Deron and I had to walk up to that platform CBS had set up, right by the Illinois people, and they were going crazy. It was such a cool feeling. That's when Deron said to me, 'Coach, this could be kind of scary if you thought about it, but once the game got started it was just a regular game."

Well, almost. After North Carolina powered past Michigan State 87-71 in the other semifinal, the game people had been talking about for months was set for Monday night. No. 1 Illinois vs. No. 2 North Carolina. Starting with the T-shirts on their backs and the logo in their locker room, Weber and his team had been planning for this moment since the season began. At last it was here.

The boy who used to play basketball in Dawn Weber's basement, the kid who liked to bang bodies at the Milwaukee rec centers and on school playgrounds while Louie Weber looked on, who listened to college basketball games under the covers late at night, the young guy naive enough to think an up-and-coming coach like Gene Keady might take a chance on him, he was standing on the doorstep of college basketball's finest stage, the one shining moment most coaches only dream about. Bruce Weber had arrived at the national championship game.

CHAPTER TWENTY-THREE

CHAMPIONSHIP GAME

A college basketball season is a marathon, not a sprint. It's a long distance run that now operates on a 12-month calendar. Nearly the moment one season ends, the next begins. That surely was the case for Illinois, when the loss in the 2004 Sweet 16 instantly focused the team on its goal of reaching the 2005 Final Four. Individual workouts in the spring are followed by grueling summers during which players are expected to work endlessly to improve their skills. School begins in August, then more individual workouts, followed by the start of team practices in mid-October. It's a cycle that never ends.

And yet with one game to go in the season of a lifetime, it felt as though the end was drawing near for Bruce Weber and his University of Illinois team. On Sunday night, the evening before the championship showdown with North Carolina, the entire Illini basketball family gathered for a final meeting. Players, coaches, families - they all assembled for a snack and a talk, and it was here, at the St.

Louis Marriott, that the finality of it all hit Weber like a sledge hammer.

"The wives and families had been a part of this for weeks now, since the post-season stuff began. Everyone was having ice cream, and kids are running around and one of my daughters said, "This is it. We aren't going to have any more meetings, are we dad?' That's when it hit me. After this there are no more games, no more meetings, no more trips. When I talked to the players that night, I had some tears. I thanked them for the year, how good they are to our families and our kids. I was just sad because there were going to be no more games, no more of what we've done. It was a high we rode through the whole thing and now it was ending."

The interaction between the players and the coaches' families was a big deal to Weber, and he appreciated the way the players showed them attention and affection. It was a sign, he felt, that his team had become a family. He even remembered the night in Atlanta, the season before at the Sweet 16, when he'd received a call from hotel security saying there had been a complaint about noise in the halls. Weber investigated and found James Augustine and Jerrance Howard playing soccer with his daughters. It no doubt reminded him of the roughhouse play he'd loved so much in Dawn Weber's house in Milwaukee, and, after he laughed at the fun they were having, he told security to chill. No harm, no foul.

At that final team meeting he scanned the faces of his players and was flooded with thoughts about each and every one. Dee Brown's pained transition and how he'd become a team player who earned Big Ten Player of the Year and All-America honors. Deron Williams and his courageous play against Arizona, how he had surely elevated himself into NBA lottery status. There was Brian Randle, who sadly missed the season with a broken hand. Randle had come to Weber more than once, including in Chicago when Luther Head was gutting it out on a gimpy hamstring, and offered to play, willing to use an entire year of eligibility just to help the team in any way. "No way I could do that to a kid," Weber said. "But he was serious about it."

Perhaps no player, though, made him prouder than Luther Head, who'd matured by leaps and bounds as a person and who Weber considered to be one of the most improved players in the country. The next night they would cry in each other's arms, but tonight

Weber recognized how far Head had come from the burglary incident to this important moment in his life. It seemed light years removed from the day Dana Brenner came to him at a social Weber was hosting for high school coaches attending his clinic and whispered, 'I need to talk to you. Some of our guys may have been involved in something.' Weber's heart sank then, but he has learned that's part of a coach's job. "If you're in this for any length of time, it's something that will happen to every coach. You're going to get a call. An accident, a speeding ticket, you hope they're not in trouble at school. But they could be. They're in college. They could be at a party and get stopped because they have beer. If you think that's not happening…. Hey, I'm a good kid from a good family, and I got in trouble. And that was when 18 was the legal drinking age in Wisconsin."

There was not much time to prepare for North Carolina, although Illinois had played the Tar Heels the previous season in Greensboro as part of the ACC/Big Ten Challenge. North Carolina won that game, 88-81, at a time when both teams were experiencing major growing pains under their first-year head coaches. "We didn't guard them and they didn't guard us," Weber recalled. "If you go back to that game, it's amazing to watch the progress of both teams. To get where we each did the next season, that's something. But we were both new - new coaches, new systems, new ways of doing things."

Weber didn't have to study much film to see why pundits were ballyhooing this game as "the best team vs. the best athletes." There was no denying the eye-popping athleticism and talent of the Tar Heels. "Our biggest concern was controlling (Raymond) Felton and their break. And, obviously, Sean May. He was so good. I thought he was playing possessed down the stretch. Just their overall size and length worried me. They were such a long team with the two Williams' (Jawad and Marvin)."

As the game drew near, the tension inside the Edward Jones Dome was building. Bill Murray was there, of course, and took Christy Weber, Bruce and Megan's middle daughter, to meet Michael Jordan, who had arrived to support his Tar Heels. The other Weber daughters, Emily and Hannah, were there as well, and Hannah wore her game face. "She's intensely competitive," Weber said of his oldest girl. "She's really into the game. She follows recruiting and stuff on the Internet." Hannah Weber is a knowledgeable and vocal fan. She learned to get on the refs by years of studying Gene Keady, the master, and even got Bob Knight to glare in her direction when she gave him a verbal lashing at the inaugural Big Ten Tournament in 1998 at the United Center in Chicago. Not bad for a young lady who was only 11 at the time.

Tension was also building in the Illini locker room, as could be expected with so much at stake. For the occasion, Weber hoped to present a quote or concept that would give his players something to think about, seizing on the "best team" theme that analysts said distinguished Illinois from North Carolina, which boasted the "best athletes." Most of all, he wanted them to remember the unselfishness and teamwork that got them here, so he turned first to Franklin D. Roosevelt, the 32nd President of the United States, and cited this quote:

"People acting together as a group can accomplish things which no individual acting alone could ever hope to bring about."

"I got it from Bill Walsh's book and the point of it was coming together and having unity. And I talked about the open hand vs. the closed fist, that North Carolina was an open hand, with five individuals, and that the fist was more powerful. I said, 'We have to be a fist tonight. We have to be powerful. We have to play like a team, because that's what we are.' I just talked about playing like we did all year, reminding them why we were good. 'Play like we play. That's what makes us special.'"

There was nothing else to say. It was time to take the court. Weber, in his customary way, exited the locker room last, alone. This time he made his way to the floor of the vibrating dome resplendent in the orange sport coat that screamed Illini and that drew a roar from the fans when they spotted him marching swiftly into view. It no doubt drew a smile from former Illini coach Lou Henson, who was seated on an aisle behind the Illini bench with his wife, Mary. Lou also wore an orange sport coat this evening, something he made famous during his 21-year tenure at Illinois. In part, Weber's wardrobe choice for the evening - something he had considered when packing back in Champaign -- was a salute to Henson and the tradition of the program.

Weber was an irritable customer on the bench from the start, and he began bristling with the referees almost immediately. Not because of calls on the court - that would come in time - but because of the way the officials were policing the two benches. North Carolina coach Roy Williams, Weber said, shared his concern.

"What really bothered me right away - and Roy said something about it, too - the refs made a big deal about the players on the bench sitting down. Several years ago they did that, saying you could cheer but you had to sit down. I thought, 'Wait a minute, we're telling our guys to cheer!' Then we make a bucket and this guy comes to me and makes a big deal out of it. I said, 'Hold on, this is the national championship game. They're not interfering with anything.' It didn't make sense to me. That was the first thing that irritated me."

But not the last, as Illinois quickly fell behind and watched as James Augustine and Deron Williams each get into early foul trouble. May's physical play in the post put Weber at odds with the officials, too. And at the same time, Illinois was having breakdowns in coverage that didn't sit well with their coach. "We gave up two layups on out-of-bounds plays, and we hadn't done that in a long time.

We failed to get back on a play because a player didn't understand his assignment, and May got a dunk on us. Roger fell on his back with a loose ball. You either hold it, get a jump ball or you're called for traveling. The worst thing you can do is throw it, and he does and they get it and get a lay-up. Then we took, I would say, five or six very uncharacteristic quick shots in the first half. When you add it up, we should have been down by about six, not 13 at the half."

The Tar Heels' 40-27 halftime lead put Illinois in a terrible bind. And when Augustine's foul troubles only escalated in the second half, defending May became a nightmarish challenge. But perhaps inspired by the comeback they'd pulled off against Arizona, Illinois made another surge, forcing fans to cinch tight their seatbelts for one final, harrowing ride.

North Carolina's lead grew to 15 points before Illinois chipped away. Moving the ball after finally solving the Tar Heels' defense, Illinois began scoring with consistency. "Coach Nottingham does the possession chart and during one timeout in the second half he said, 'Well, I have good news and bad news. The good news is we've scored on nine of 10 possessions. The bad news is we've only cut five points off their lead.' I looked at him and said, 'That means they're pretty good, huh.' We'd made a run, but it didn't get us much.

"When a team like that gets you to double digits you'd think we might quit, but we didn't. And they got stagnant." Sure enough, Illinois came all the way back - not once, but twice - first tying the game 65-65 on a pair of free throws by Dee Brown with 5:34 to play, then doing it again at 70-70 on Luther Head's 3-point basket with 2:40 to go. On that shot, CBS showed Megan Weber throwing her head back in glee, and every Illinois fan on the planet was praying for one more Arizona-like miracle.

Two shots killed that dream. One was a dagger of a 3-pointer by Felton that wrestled the lead back to the Tar Heels with 5:10 to play. The other was an acrobatic tip by the freshman, Marvin Williams, after Rashad McCants missed a wild drive to the hoop. "Felton's pull-up three was an unbelievable shot," Weber said. "Then they shoot a bad, double-pump lay-up that Roy is so mad about he takes his guy out of the game. And it gets tipped in." Williams' tip with 1:27 remaining put North Carolina ahead for good, 72-70.

Still, Illinois had a chance. Three open 3-pointers in the closing seconds all bounced away. "Deron had one and Luther had two," Weber said. "All three looked like they were going in. I know in the first half we took some bad threes, but we were 6 of 11 or 7 of 11 to start the second half before missing the last four or five. Still, I never would have thought we'd shoot 40 threes."

As Carolina hit its free throws in the closing seconds, Weber realized the dream would finish one game short. At the conclusion of North Carolina's 75-70 victory, confetti rained from the top of the dome, and the Tar Heel players whooped it up along with their coach, Roy Williams, who had finally broken through in the title game. "I started walking down to shake hands with Roy, but they're all hugging and I'm not going to bother them. That's their moment. I understood perfectly. I felt like a lonely guy among 47,000 people. So I just headed for our locker room."

Williams quickly realized he had missed Weber. "All of a sudden Wayne McClain came running and said, 'Roy wants you.'" Williams practically sprinted off the court to catch Weber and was gracious in his praise. "He said, 'I've been here. I know what it's like. I'm sorry

I didn't shake your hand right away. You guys had an unbelievable year. It was just amazing how your kids came back.' He was really nice."

In the locker room there was a predictable collection of fierce disappointment, deep sadness, a little anger and some regret. It was the sadness and regret Weber wanted swept away. "I told them, 'There's nothing to be sad about guys. We lost. We lost to a very good team. You played your hearts out and came back. You came back two times when no one would have given you a chance. The only thing to be sad about is that we can't do this again." And with that, Weber hugged and thanked each of his seniors, crying as he wrapped himself around each one. The sadness of a journey ended had now sunk in.

On his way to the post-game press conference, Weber crossed paths with Lou and Mary Henson, who were being transported in a golf cart. "It was neat to see him," Weber said. "He hugged me, and I talked with them both."

When the team left the dome together, Weber was asked how he wanted them to enter the Marriott, where hordes of fans had gathered. Through a back entrance? Dodging the masses? "No, I told them we wanted to go in through the main lobby. These guys deserved it. There were tons of people, people on the street, beeping horns, getting out of their cars."

The players made their way through the crowd, most of them finding their families and scattering for some late night food. Weber went to a banquet room where he was joined by his wife and daughters, by brothers Ron and David and sister Jan and their families, and by a number of nieces and nephews. "It was kind of neat," he said. "We just sat there eating, talking about the game, talking about my mom. Some of my buddies from Milwaukee were there. I remember we didn't come out of there until 2 or 2:30, and people were still in the lobby." Finally, Weber retreated to his room. Thoughts, vivid images and deep emotions ricocheted through his brain, making sleep nearly impossible. One undeniable thought kept reoccurring: The season of a lifetime was over.

CHAPTER TWENTY-FOUR

POSTSCRIPT

A welcome home celebration was planned for the next day in Champaign where thousands of fans hoped to turn out to greet the national champs. But after coming up short in the title game, Weber was certain no one felt much like celebrating. "I told Rod Cardinal, 'No one's going to come. Maybe we should just cancel it.'"

But fans began arriving early, just as they did for games, dressed in orange and led by loyalty. "We're on the bus and people were still on the highway overpass on the way back. Then we make the turn onto Neil Street, and people were on the street, coming out of their stores. It was special. And now we start getting close, and there are cars everywhere. I couldn't believe it and neither could our guys."

Inside Memorial Stadium, where a sea of orange filled the west stands and spilled into the horseshoe, thunderous applause greeted each player as he was introduced. "The first couple of guys who stepped out said, 'There's 20,000 or 25,000 people out there.' That was really neat. That was a great finish to the year, and it was very rewarding to the kids."

Among the dignitaries on hand, perhaps no one delivered a more appropriate message than the university's chancellor, Dr. Richard Herman, who reassured the players by saying, "You didn't let us down. You lifted us up."

"Then we came back to Ubben, and I'll bet James, Dee, Roger and some of the other guys signed autographs for two, two-and-a-half hours. The next day I came in because we had scheduled visits with recruits. They had called and said under the circumstances, we did-n't have to come. But these are Chicago kids, and we've tried to make a commitment to them, so we're going.

"When I got to the office, Jay Price had film on and he said, 'You have to watch this,' and we looked at some of the plays, some of the calls from the North Carolina game. The whole way driving to Chicago I would have these uncontrollable fits of cussing, and Jay would just laugh. Now everything is running through your mind for the first time. I remember pulling into the parking lot of the school we visited. Jay said, 'Coach, you can't just start cussing during the visit.'"

Weber hopes there's a lasting impact from a season that seemed to make an impression on the nation. "You hope that recruiting-wise it will help. You have your name out there. Now people know my face. They know our program. We became a national product. Certain programs, whether it's Kentucky, Carolina or Duke, they've been a national product for 10, 15, 25 years. People don't understand it's not instant. But I hope we can use this as a builder for the program.

"I think it was amazing that it happened in our 100th season. I think we brought people back together. I think we brought the state on board. My goal is that every kid in the state wants to come to Illinois. Every kid can't come, because sometimes you have three shooting guards in your program and you can't take three more. And not everyone is an academic qualifier. But the kids who want to come and who we have a position for, I hope we bring them all. It's going to come over the course of time. You wish it was easier, but it's still hard. Jim Calhoun told me the Final Four appearance really doesn't benefit you until the second year. Kids make their decisions so much earlier and a lot of times they narrow their choices as sophomores and juniors. You just hope someone latches on to us. We're not sure who that is now, but it will help us down the road."

Weber also hopes the lasting legacy of this team is a style of play that becomes the personality of all future Illini teams. "We played it at Southern Illinois, but you don't get watched, and you don't have the athletes to do it to the max. It's a style kids like to play. It promotes freedom and originality yet it relies on team play. And I know the fans like it."

It's a style that Weber relates to something he calls "sharing the juices." When going on the road, visiting teams will find a limited number of juice bottles available for players at halftime. "They know exactly how many players we have," Weber said. "If it's 13, there will be 13 bottles of juice in there. None for the coaches.

When I got here, the first guy through the door would take four. He'd put one in his locker, one in his bag, one in his warm-up and the other he'd drink. The next guy would take three. And before long, there were none left for the other guys.

"I told them if they're going to be a team, they have to learn to share the juices. Not only does the first guy take just one, but he makes sure the next guy has one, right down to the last player in the room. If you share the juices you'll share the basketball."

Weber said he learned this lesson the hard way. "I was from a family of seven with five kids and my parents. There are eight slices in a pizza, and you had to eat fast to get a second slice of pizza. We didn't share the juices at our house. I hadn't learned that yet. I learned to hide a slice of pizza under my napkin. But sharing the juices is what this team did on the basketball court. We shared the basketball as well as anyone. We set a standard, not only for Illinois basketball but nationally. We had success because we shared the juices.

"You can't play defense with only four guys guarding. Everyone has to guard. You have to share the workload. You have to share the juices." The ultimate "share the juices" example was the possession against Northwestern when Illinois made 15 passes before Dee Brown drained a three. "I remember getting mad, saying, 'Shoot it! You're open, shoot it! Shoot it!' And they kept passing. When Dee took that three you just knew it was going in." Ironically, when North Carolina coach Roy Williams needed to give his team a lesson in unselfish play, he showed them a film clip of how it's done. The play? Illinois' 15-pass masterpiece against the Wildcats.

As the season wound down, after the team banquet and after he had dealt with Deron Williams and Dee Brown and their professional aspirations, Weber could at long last begin reflecting on the season and on the sliver of peace and quiet that should come his way in the off-season. Perhaps there would be a family vacation to Marco Island in Florida, where Bruce and Megan Weber shared their honeymoon and where they have returned nearly every year since. "All of our girls learned to swim there. We'd take them when they were two or three, throw them in the water and they'd learn how to swim. And we go in the summer when it's like a desolate community. If you're looking for a lot of action, that's probably not your place. It's too slow. But all we want to do is lay on the beach."

And in August, the Weber family planned to hold a reunion at sister Jan Moeller's home in Frankfort, near Joliet. That will be the time - away from the surreal glare of a basketball season that became so public - for the Webers to finally pay homage to their mother, Dawn Weber.

When she passed away on March 11, 2005, the incredible Orange Krush student section decided to take action in her honor. So they earmarked money pledged for 3-point baskets over the final nine games of the season to a fund in Dawn Weber's name. "They gave us the money to use at our discretion," Bruce Weber said. "What I'd like to do is take that money and in my mother's and father's names, endow a scholarship for our team managers because they don't have that now. This will be the initial down payment. I've always thought my parents served people and that's what team managers do. My parents were givers. The managers are givers. The only thing they take is the enjoyment of being part of it." The Orange Krush donation: More than $125,000.

When Bruce Weber's father, Louie, died 18 years ago last October, the family returned from the funeral only to find out their home had been broken into. "People were watching the obituaries in the newspaper and robbing homes during the times listed for the funeral service," Weber said. Thankfully, Dawn Weber's funeral brought a different response.

Even though she no longer lived in the family home in Milwaukee - the one where Bruce Weber cracked his head on the basement beam - friends leaving the funeral service drove by the old home and tossed flowers onto the lawn and the front walk. It was their way of saying they remembered, that they cared. "The neighborhood had kind of gotten run down, and I wonder what those people must have thought," Weber said.

He has been inundated by gestures of kindness from fans who want him to know how special the 2004-05 Illini season was for them. When he checked into the hotel in St. Louis at the Final Four, he was greeted with all kinds of gifts, including flowers, chocolate basketballs and throat lozenges sent from a fan in Europe who heard he'd lost his voice after the comeback against Arizona.

Someone even sent him the lucky pillow they sat on during that memorable game. After the season was over, when Weber was in a Santa Monica, California, airport wearing nothing that would distinguish him as having Illini ties, a fan raced up and babbled breathlessly, "Coach Weber, that was the most unforgettable game I've ever seen!"

"I know it was a season that touched a lot of people," Weber says now. "It was really kind of unbelievable."

The history books will say the 100th year of University of Illinois basketball was the winningest season of all time. They'll say an unselfish team led by second-year coach Bruce Weber became the school's first to reach the national championship game. They'll say fans followed this team in record numbers, that orange became the benchmark color of Illini Nation, that something magical occurred on a journey two years in the making.

Only those who lived it - who felt the emotion of it - understand it was so much more than that.